3.6
LEADERSHIP

3.6

LEADERSHIP

Leadership to Build Personal and Career Success

Charles Farrior

3.6 LEADERSHIP
LEADERSHIP TO BUILD PERSONAL AND CAREER SUCCESS

iUniverse books may be ordered through booksellers or by contacting:

iUniverse
1663 Liberty Drive
Bloomington, IN 47403
www.iuniverse.com
1-800-Authors (1-800-288-4677)

Because of the dynamic nature of the Internet, any web addresses or links contained in this book may have changed since publication and may no longer be valid. The views expressed in this work are solely those of the author and do not necessarily reflect the views of the publisher, and the publisher hereby disclaims any responsibility for them.

Any people depicted in stock imagery provided by Thinkstock are models, and such images are being used for illustrative purposes only.
Certain stock imagery © Thinkstock.

ISBN: 978-1-5320-3131-1 (sc)
ISBN: 978-1-5320-3130-4 (e)

Library of Congress Control Number: 2017915036

Print information available on the last page.

iUniverse rev. date: 01/31/2018

Contents

Part 5 – Avoid The Maze

Part 6 – Keeping on the High Road to Success

WHERE ARE YOU HEADING?

I have taught and presented many leadership topics over the years as a Manager, but 3.6 Leadership has to stand out for me. There have been more follow-up responses and requests for it to be taught in more detail than other themes I have presented. As one of the more popular leadership topics, the intent of this book is put the ideas of the concept into an easily understandable thought and management model – with the focus on tailoring it with memory cues for ease of recall, while integrating it into an expanded holistic personal and career perspective. Specifically, I will drive into more salient detail about these leadership concepts for application.

My experiences in mentoring is also relevant for this exploration and discussion. I have had the privilege and opportunity to mentor dozens of professionals over my career. As such, one of the first things I try to do when the mentoring sessions start is to determine where the person is in their life and career. I am not talking about what their official position is. Going into mentoring with a person I already know that. But what is their outlook, and why do they think what they think? What is it they want to accomplish? Do they believe they are on track? If so, why? If not, why? Do they have a plan? If so, how is it recorded?

I have also recently attained my certification for leadership coaching through the Eagle Center for Leadership. Conceptually, the approach is again to ask questions. But it is even more focused in leading the coachee to identify those areas needing change, and for them to also identify a specific plan of action to accomplish the change. Accountability of the coachee's progress to that change goal is a key part of the coaching.

What about You? Why are you doing what you are doing? Many people choose a job out of college with the basic idea of "I have to get a job." Certainly that is true for most, but the search in many cases has no focus and no point other than just get a job. The same can be said if you are coming off of a layoff. Those circumstances are definitely some of the most stressful.

Obviously, you need to get work and sometimes the match is not perfect. But that does not mean that you should not have a plan, a mission, and direction. You do not have to settle for what seems to be second best indefinitely.

This book is designed to help you define your purpose and your mission, with some useful tips which will make these principles come to life for you, and to find the right job that will help you fulfill your personal passion and support your family. Even if you are not in that perfect job yet, you still need to experience success. This book will help you at every stop.

PART 1

GETTING TO KNOW YOURSELF

Chapter 1

YOUR MISSION

During the first meeting with a mentee, I usually give them two or three action items to accomplish before our second meeting. These action items are related to their career and path forward. I also usually include asking them to read or to begin to read *The 7 Habits of Highly Effective People* (Covey, 2013) if they have not already done so. At one of my former managerial assignments, when I had interns graduating out of the intern program, I bought them the *7 Habits* book as a gift. I viewed it as vital that those entering the professional phase of their career should begin exposing themselves to a leadership and development culture that could help shape their future.

In addition to offering instruction on becoming efficient and effective professionals with certain interpersonal habits, the book focuses first on challenging readers to write a personal mission statement, as well as gaining a basic understanding of communication and emotional bank accounts. This also serves as a good indication to me about how serious the mentee is with improving their personal outlook for their professional career. If they are willing to invest just a little bit of time and effort now to focus on their personal mission, it would pay tremendous dividends for their future career success.

Not one of those mentored had ever written a personal mission statement before our mentoring sessions. That does not mean they were bad people with poor intentions - quite the opposite. Virtually all of them meant well and wanted to do great work with superior end products, and were in varying stages of accomplishing those work products. They just had not been challenged to look at their career in the context of their life's total mission and goals.

This knowledge and exercise is critical to understand where you are heading. What path is the right path? What company can serve as the platform to assist you in fulfilling your desired career path and mission, while you are supplying effort to make that company successful in its ventures? Are you actually in the right job with the right company?

When first discussing the need to have a mission statement with the mentees, many of them thought it was referring to their mission at work. They were theorizing and espousing what their job responsibilities were and how that was important to their organization. That view is not unexpected. Most business theories in formal educational settings discuss organizational structure and the mission which the organization uses as its business compass without tying in the personal element. Understanding how you fit into your company's mission is important. That was also my initial thought when I read the Covey book for the first time over 20 years ago. I thought the mission statement was related to the organization only. That is how it had always been contextualized and presented to me.

But the mission statement in discussion here is more of a perspective that addresses the entire individual, both professional and personal. What drives the person? What are the priorities of the person? How are close family members, personal causes, and work tied together in the mission statement to provide that clear life focus and direction for the individual?

If your personal life is not driving your compass, you will find that there will always be a conflict. That is a conflict that will tear at you, both professionally and personally. When I say personally in this context, you also must think about your family and family relationships. The last thing you need to do is to embark on a career that leaves your family behind physically or emotionally while you are pursuing professional accomplishments. Applying all of your life focus and energy on your job will leave your family in the dark wondering when you will come home and will wonder when their relationships will matter to you. Please do not underestimate the importance of this. This is a priority that will be a game changer for your future.

In Brian Houston's book of *Live Love Lead* (Houston, 2015), he asks "What are your strengths?" Sometimes when you are prioritizing your life's activities this is ignored. It does not mean that you should put only strengths, or consider only strengths when crafting your mission statement. But you should not ignore your key capabilities. Potentially you may wind up identifying areas which may be considered as weaknesses if they tie into one of your personal passions. That is perfectly acceptable, and in many cases logical.

Defining your mission statement really takes significant reflection. It is sometimes easy to just put down what you have been doing in the past, rather than trying to determine where you are heading in the future. The reason for that is what you have experienced is what you know the best. They include both successes and failures. It does not mean that you either like or dislike it. It is just more comfortable dealing with the known than the unknown. Where do you see your family in five years? Where do you see your career in five years? What about 20 years? Are your strengths in communicating with other people? Are your weaknesses in communicating, or something else? In any case, these are weighty issues one should consider when composing their mission statement.

When I first took on the job of writing my mission statement it was difficult to see beyond five or ten years. I was having a hard enough time seeing out just a few months. I wound up stating mission statement goals that ran onto a second page. I believe there were approximately 15 goals I listed. That is a lot of goals, and the focus was somewhat questionable, though, well-meaning. Today there are five goals supporting my mission statement.

Your personal life should be front and center in your mission statement. Without the success of your personal life, it will be more of a challenge to be successful professionally. Not impossible – but more difficult and **nearly** impossible. But don't be fooled into believing you could be the exception to that statement. Your family needs you.

When viewed in the context of family and personal causes, it is very easy to understand how integral the mission statement is to determine how well your current professional status matches your stated priorities and values. It will capture your passion. Your mission lays out your path and values, but your vision (I call it passion) leads you into the future. This is necessary to determine the next steps.

A lot of organizations get hung up on terminology, but just like in accounting, the primary consideration this side of the legal line is to be consistent. What may be overhead to one company could be G&A to another. What may be G&A to another company could be a direct charge by the next. You just need to be consistent and document your approach.

Similarly, a company may choose to have a vision. That is a positive – (remember I call it passion). Call it what you would like. However, I believe the term "passion" more accurately covers the description. Your passion will drive you and everything you do. If you have lost your passion, you definitely need to refocus your passion on your personal mission and life and regain it.

Chapter 2

THE RIGHT JOB

Are you already in the right job for your career, or do you believe that you need to be in another job? The answer to that question is huge, and it may not be easy to answer. That conclusion can be affected by a number of factors such as the goals you have identified as part of your mission statement and career plan. Think of it like this. Your mission statement is your overarching list of things which are important to you. Your passion and career plan are roadmaps to get you there.

Also, have you been exposed to new processes, customers, or products in your current job and are you still being exposed to new projects, or is everything repetitive? Sometimes things are not always black and white when you make these assessments. Sometimes the scope of innovation and outcomes, as well as culture driven by leadership or management, affects the overall assessment of how much you are growing or excelling in your current job. If you are continually learning and experiencing success in a positive culture, perhaps you are already in the right job for this season of your life. It is thought provoking for sure, and it is deep reflection that should occur.

Initially, though, for this early discussion I am going to make the assumption you have concluded that you need to be in a new job and you feel up to the challenge of the job search. More on the right job issue later.

Several years ago I had the opportunity to hear Dr. Malcolm Portera speak several times over a period of approximately four years. Dr. Portera has served, among other positions, as President of Mississippi State University and Chancellor of the University of Alabama System, which includes the University of Alabama in Tuscaloosa, the University of Alabama in Huntsville, and the University of Alabama at Birmingham. One of the things that impressed me so much about Dr. Portera was that when he presented to an audience, he ensured he would make either three or four very specific points – never more than that, and never less. He wanted to stay concise, connect with the audience, and ensure that his message was received. He knew those points frontwards and backwards. He didn't need the monitor feedback of his PowerPoint slides to make sure he remembered the points and associated details. Very impressive and always a strong presentation.

Similarly, as we walk thru the discussion of pursuing career excellence and in the right job, I want to lay out three requirements for strong resumes, and three requirements for strong interviews. If you do these three things, for each, you are guaranteed your likelihood of accomplishing success in your search will increase very significantly. It is easier than you think, and probably harder than you thought or hoped if you have not given it much thought. I have hired hundreds of employees in my career and I have seen a lot of things in the hiring process in both resumes and interviews. While some are the "best of" practices, many of them are not so pretty. Some even borderline on the absurd.

There are too many people who approach finding a job with a jaded view. Some view getting a job like finding a needle in a haystack – so why even try or offer little effort; or some think that "since this was what I was taught in a business class 20 years ago I am going to stick with that approach". Well – if you haven't noticed, at least a couple of things have changed in the world over the last 20 years – or 10 years or 5 years, or even since last year. Since 1997, we have had four Presidents, Y2K, 9/11, the Global War on Terror, scandals, overall poor economic climate with cyclical variations, and an incredible leap in technology platforms. It is primarily the latter that is allowing the talent management community to do things quicker on totally different platforms than what was the norm. Those organizations that fail to keep up with these advances tend to fail or falter in organizational effectiveness.

The Missing Link. Before elaborating on "resume requirements", I want to specify more on some of the changes which are evident today. First, LinkedIn has become the primary job search engine for talent management personnel to identify potential candidates for jobs. If you do not have a LinkedIn profile which is current and up to date, you have completely missed the boat. This is what the majority of recruiters or headhunters are using today to screen for candidates for their jobs. Resumes are also used in this process. It is imperative to have both fronts covered here.

There are many instructional videos on YouTube to assist you in setting up a profile. However, personal research to get "best-of" practices cannot be emphasized enough. You must stay current and you must stay active in the LinkedIn community. It should be a parallel to your resume. Some say it is an online version of your resume. A primary difference can be LinkedIn is chronologically driven. There are many in the talent management field who prefer a capability resume versus one that is chronologically driven. I will discuss the resume in just a bit.

LinkedIn also allows you to establish an online personal brand. This is important and will play into the concept of Leadership Marketing. You will have the opportunity to expand also into your charitable and volunteer efforts where you have displayed leadership, and also it gives you the opportunity to write thought pieces and post them for consumption by the LinkedIn community. This gives you the forum to immediately post information which may be relevant to others for thought or product/process consideration. This all takes place without having to gain the approval of an editorial board of a periodical which sometimes hangs up posting articles in their magazine or publication with delays. Therefore, make good use of being able to post your thought pieces on LinkedIn as it furthers your personal brand, and also gives you the opportunity to put your writing style on display. What do you bring to the table for your prospective employer? LinkedIn should answer that, as well as your resume.

Second, the real secret of LinkedIn, though, is your professional connections. Too often we meet people, lose their business cards and never invest time to maintain relationships. It is those relationships and contacts which generate most job opportunities.

I (2017 July 13) posted an article on LinkedIn entitled, "Who Will Take Your Box?" In it I tell the story about when I was leaving one of my former organizations. The person who came by to wish me well at the end of my last full day was the CFO of the company with which I conducted a significant portion of my business and negotiations. Based on respect and relationship, the CFO insisted on walking out with me on my last trip out of the building and carry the last box I had. He insisted over my (mild) protests. Sometimes it is just appropriate to say "thank you". It was just one professional being nice to another, with no strings attached.

Staying In Touch. The second part of the story, though, was that I didn't keep in touch with him, and to this day I have lost total contact on his whereabouts. I had changed organizations in a different state and I had hit the ground running – too busy really to do what I should have done (or so I reasoned). You should always stay in touch with former friends and professional associates. It just is good business and professional practice that should be kept up. Remember those contacts can generate opportunities for you. Maybe it is not an opportunity of a job, but perhaps it is the discussion of a problem with the result a generation of ideas or solutions, or the introduction of a person. Moreover, the richness of friendships and relationships are even stronger than the "what is in it for me" perspective. You can absolutely never have too many friends. That is one thing I tell my son all the time. Make friends and stay in touch with them. There are too many available communication and social platforms to let people slip into the pages of history instead of staying in touch.

I have heard in talent management circles that only one in five, to one in eight or nine jobs are filled through formal job announcements. There are always exceptions to any rule of thumb – and five years from now the discussion will have changed again. The point, though, is relationships and communication will be key to you finding the right job. This has been and will always be true no matter what stage of your career you find yourself.

PART 2

THE RIGHT TOOLS
FOR YOUR SEARCH

Chapter 3

TIP #1 FOR RESUMES - IMPRESSION

The first tip for resumes is the Impression. You have no more than 10 seconds to make an impression. Will yours be positive or negative? Some in the talent management community often state you have only six seconds in a resume review. I know that I have heard Dr. Dawn Graham say that on the Wharton Business Radio channel, and she is one of the most respected practitioners in the HR community. I have heard others also say this, but with Dr. Graham, the Director of Career Management in the MBA Program at the Wharton School, the credibility is tremendously high. I strongly recommend you listen to her on that channel if you either are in the job market, or you desire to stay current on new trends in human capital. Even if you do not have a satellite receiver in your vehicle you can download and subscribe on your mobile device. Common practices change frequently so take advantage of free job-search tools and advice.

There are also other career "hacks" which can be found on that channel. Just for clarity "hacks" represents a shortcut with a position spin towards efficiency. Last Century it meant something totally different. It was referring to usually negative subjects or actions (e.g. the burglar hacked into the safe; that guy was a hack). Remember times are changing....

How Long Should It Be? When doing a resume review for rating purposes, I found for each additional page it doubles your review time. For example, a two-page resume would take three minutes (one for the first, and two for the second). A three-page resume would take six minutes, and a four-page resume would take 10 to 12 minutes. This is meant to be a generalization to a certain extent. Complexity and number of resumes will affect your time. When writing your resume, some say you should never go back more than 20 years of listed experience on a resume – and some say 10 years. Depending on the type of work you do, if you go back too far in experience it may be deemed irrelevant. Recruiters are interested in what you have done lately.

The real answer is it all depends. It depends on if it is a management job or one that is technically driven. Is it a job that only requires one year of experience or an intern program? Does it require a lot of experience, or the ability to show potential? There is not a clear answer to that.

First Impression is Key? What is clear is your resume needs to be concise and it needs to make a quick positive impression. Even if a full resume review is required which thoroughly looks at each item listed, would you prefer the first point of reference or impression be positive or negative? That is a big question. Obviously, you would prefer positive. A positive impression will start the reviewer(s) scan of your resume on the right foot.

You usually cannot recover from a negative first impression. In a situation where there are many applications and resumes, the reviewer or review team looks for quick ways to narrow the search to find those worth further consideration. This is not a point in which you should be afraid. Just do what you need to do to put the best foot forward.

Up front state your key skills (e.g. creator, leader, problem solver, process improvement expert, engineering manager, experienced project manager). This should not be more than two lines, and it should be designed to set the table of expectations for the resume review or perusal and it should give an idea of the type of value the reviewer will see in your resume. The reviewer is trying to determine if the applicant will add value to their organization.

Chapter 4

TIP #2 FOR RESUMES – THE SO WHAT

The next tip for resumes seems rather obvious. However, apparently, it is not. The applicant often submits resumes and it shows a lot of activity, but not much on accomplishments. There are several pitfalls in writing your resumes and they are included here for reference.

Don't Do This. When you write your resume – cut out the "I". I have read resumes that essentially say – (I came to work. I worked on teams. I did my job. I accomplished my assignments. I satisfied customers. I trained others, etc. – ad nauseum). Ugghh – No! Don't do that. Some people are advised to do this for some unknown reason. In my debriefings I have heard, "Well Johnny Joe and Sally Sue said to do that." Resume readers are time limited. If you want your resume details read, don't do this.

"I" in the resume world is the counterpart of "you" being understood in some English sentences. For example - "Go get the water." "Please answer the door." The subject of both of those sentences is "you". When you revert to the "I did" approach, you are also conveying that you cannot communicate in an intelligible and educated fashion. If you cannot communicate, business leaders and managers do not need you or want you. Those managers who are accountable for products which are time sensitive do not need someone who cannot convey simple and concise thoughts. It is not going to help them accomplish their assigned missions. Ultimately, your choice is listen to Johnny Joe and Sally Sue, or write a professional resume and have it read with a positive outlook. Doing the former will hurt your selection chances; doing the latter will help them. As the Knight protecting the Holy Grail in *Indiana Jones and the Last Crusade* said, "Choose wisely." (You is the subject in that sentence also.)

Or This. Also, while I am at it – do not copy your position description or another position description into your resume. It is a worthless waste of time. Resume readers see that and instantly view the writer as someone who has no initiative or self-awareness. People ask me, do people really do that? Unfortunately, the answer is yes. They are from a school of thought that a pound of paper increases the likelihood of being picked for a job. I can promise you that nothing is further from the truth. When someone does that it only angers the reviewer because their time is being wasted. Good things do not occur when you anger a reviewer!

So What. Now You Should Do This. However, if you can identify you provided a solution a week early, and consequently helped a customer solve their long-running logistical problem while saving them $1M/year and $50K for getting it to them early, that will resonate with the resume reviewer. That would be a great example of the "so what" in this case.

Including the "so what" is critical. If the reviewer is looking for someone who can prospectively accomplish certain things in their office such as providing customer service, they are not looking for someone to just say "provided customer service". They are looking for someone who has experience in providing and can explain concisely (think one line) what they did and what the resulting impact was.

"Provided customer service" says nothing. "Led emergency repair of XYZ production line machinery within 2 hours, and maintained customer schedule," says a lot. It shows what you did, how fast you did it, and the result of it. It is concise, and the reviewer understands completely what the "so what" is and whether it matches their need. Don't leave out the "so what". Even if you have a connection and potential inside track, a sloppy resume could result in your connection getting a chink in their reputation and may result in you getting removed from consideration.

Chapter 5

TIP #3 FOR RESUMES – YOU ARE

Who Are You? After you finish your resume, your intended resume reader should know who you are. Back up a minute. Back up and see if you can determine who you are. Get a couple of people to read (in confidence) your resume and ask them what your resume describes. If you have described yourself as someone with a lot of business development success and you want a job as a lead engineer or a project engineer with no experience in those areas depicted, there is a disconnect. You have to decide how to tell that story in words. What do your courtesy readers of your resume tell you about this. Similarly, if they are unclear on what you are conveying, perhaps you did not get the "so what" down well enough. These dots start to connect very quickly, and they will all affect how successful you are in your job hunt.

Tailor Your Resume. You may have a great impression up front, and have outstanding "so what's", but you must describe what the resume reader needs to see. Tailoring your resume to a job is recommended where practical. If you want the job bad enough to put in for it, do a little more work on identifying and bringing out the quality of experience that matches the job requisition or announcement. That has been shown to yield a much higher match probability for candidates.

Be Consistent. Your resume also needs to be consistent with your LinkedIn profile. That does not mean your resume has to be in a chronological format like LinkedIn. Tailor it in a way that best defines you meeting the job requirement. In many cases a functional resume is the absolute best way to go, because it is focusing on your matched skillsets and accomplishments. That is even more true the more experience and more jobs you have. Several jobs with their own fenced off areas on the resume tend to eat up space, and no one wants to read a resume that is the length of a diary. If you are on your second job with less than five years' experience it may be difficult to transition to a functional resume. Again, that is a generality by the fact that you have had just two jobs with somewhat limited experience. Clarity of your information is key in all cases.

Who Are You? Another aspect in defining yourself, you need to do some type of personality indication test such as Myers-Briggs (MB). It can reveal important self-awareness characteristics. However, it occasionally may be difficult to remember your personality type or designator because there are so many personality dimensions and types. Personally, I am ENTJ. That means Extraversion, Intuition, Thinking, and Judging. Over time your perspective can also change as I was an ESTJ. The movement from Sensing (or fact based) to futuristic views and planning does not mean that I do not care for facts. My experiential perspective had changed, though. On another survey that I took only about a year and a half prior to the MB survey, it concluded that I was very uncomfortable unless I knew all the facts. It deduced that I felt safe operationally when all of the rules were clearly stated. What they missed in their assessment was why I wanted the facts. Once I have facts in hand, it was then that I could come up with a strategy and solution – even if it had never been tried before. Also, on the second MB test, the degree of Extraversion had gone down. Therefore, it is safe to say that depending on your life experiences and views which may evolve over time, this could easily affect your classification. That is not a bad thing; it is just an observation.

Another personality test I found particularly useful was in *Make a Difference* (Little, 2013). It breaks the personality traits into four quadrants, that of the Monkey, Lion, Camel, and Turtle. By answering several questions presented in the book, you can find out what your dominant personality trait is, along with your secondary trait.

It is much easier to understand the relationships you have in your life if you understand yourself and have the information to be aware of personality differences with those with whom you interact. That could be applicable for relationships in the office or at home. By understanding relationships and differences in people, you have a better idea on how to communicate with them and sometimes give them space to process information or issues. This should yield more productive and effective relationships. Frankly, if you do not have effective relationships at home and at work – you are in trouble!

In summary, the three requirements for a successful resume are-

Impression

So What

You Are

Chapter 6

INTERVIEW TIP #1 – WHY?

You need to clearly understand why you are going on an interview. The most obvious reason is to get another job. A second primary, but less used, reason is to get experience interviewing.

There may be a third reason that is rarely used, and that is for leverage for their current company to gain increased potential favorable consideration for more responsibility, prime assignments, or an increase in salary. Some say this latter case is risky, and I will address this reason first. I recently participated in a discussion on LinkedIn regarding this, and there were several differing opinions. The biggest negative on this, apparently, was some believed that they could lose out by their current employer basically severing ties with you because you got another offer. Then others expressed that your current employer would make life hard for you because you "appear" to not be loyal.

Is There Risk? Personally, I see no risk in it. If you go on an interview you should be ready to go to a new job. Interviews are great experiences and something can be learned about yourself in each case. If your current employer is ready to cut ties with you because you go on an interview, is that a place you really want to work? Not only is that company's attitude to that employee disrespectful, it is showing the hand of the company culture. If they treat one person like that, you can rest assured the company is treating others the same way. Rarely does a company behave inconsistently in employee treatment. If an organization does not want you, you do not want to be there.

Many years ago, I successfully employed this strategy. I was ready to go to a new employer in a different city and we actually looked at housing options. But when I went to my then-current management after my offer (they knew I was interviewing in advance), they decided they would make it worth my while to stay. I was very glad they did. I actually loved the job and the people. The mission was great, the culture and people were great – the money just was not great or acceptable for my personal circumstances. If you are not used to having conversations with a degree of tact, there is never a better time to learn than when you are in this situation. It is just a conversation, and it is your future. If you do not look out for yourself and family, you cannot expect someone else to do it.

This is a way to find out how much your current organization values you and your talents. But you do need to open yourself up to the idea of actually leaving if you choose the interview for this purpose.

Historical Context. Back on point - in the 1900's, until the latter part of the Century, most people stayed at one employer their whole career. That is just how it was done. Lifestyles were totally different. One company; one pension system; one gold watch at retirement. However, with the shift in pension systems to where individuals now have primary responsibility for their future retirement pension and benefits, most people change jobs several times during their career. With married couples having both spouses working most of the time, it actually provides an income and benefits safety net for frequent job changes. There are more alternatives in trying to protect the family unit financially. Should there be just one income earner, though, it makes for a little less margin for error.

Taking Care of Yourself. In large part, individuals are compelled to take care of themselves and their families. Recently I heard that millennials can be expected to change jobs 10 times during their career. Those who are pre-millennial can also change jobs 10 or more times during their career if they are following their personal mission and passion.

Personally, I am a pre-millennial with millennial tendencies and I can check that box of changing jobs at least 10 times and have many tremendous outcomes, accomplishments, and relationships at every stop, every locale, and every organization. There are pro's and con's with moving several times and supporting different organizations. Among other things you gain so many different rich experiences, relationships, and perspectives. But, you have to decide what your personal mission is and what is best for you and your family. That should be the thing that drives your passion and mission.

The reality is when you leave your job (doesn't matter which one), someone else will come in behind you and assume that responsibility. Unfortunately, over time you see people with whom you work suddenly die. While this is a terrible thing to witness in the workplace, it is part of life. You lose a friend and a co-worker and then what?

Someone will have to immediately step up and take over those responsibilities. Since everyone, including you, is replaceable, your primary focus should be what is best for you and your family. Keep the right priority as you are struggling with working 10 or 12 hours a day. If you are working 12 hours a day, what do you think your priority is? What if you are traveling three weeks out of every four on a repetitive basis? Actions speak louder than words. Remember, you are replaceable at work – no matter the reason.

Companies Value Productive Employees. Companies view employees leaving in a variety of ways. But for certain, companies should arm themselves with the information relating to the cost of losing an employee. Employees need to understand this also. Reports over the years have shown that an organization losing a person can cause the organization to experience costs ranging from 100% to 200% of their annual salary (Heathfield, 2010). That is dependent on a range of factors including experience, industry, and product output to the company. Wayne Cascio concluded with similar findings. (Cascio, Young, & Morris, 1997). Christina Merhar also recently verified that depending on some of the factors listed above the costs can range from as little as approximately 20% for unskilled high turnover labor to over 200% for highly skilled and hard to fill positions. (2016). It is clear from a bottom-line perspective that it is in the best interest of the organization to keep a productive employee from a production and cost mitigation standpoint, rather than let him or her go, if at all possible.

However, it is important for the reader to understand what factors may be in play as he or she is trying to determine if an organization is the right employer to stay and support. Alternatively, it may provide useful information leading to an individual who wants to pursue a new job with a new employer. In a previous article I published on human resource costing pertaining to job losses (2003), I compiled 12 factors impacting employee reduction calculations to ensure total accountability of factors would be considered by companies when calculating costs for human resource reductions. The reason is that many companies either reflexively or instinctively just cut the human labor variable cost if they need quick reductions in costs. There is usually no analysis or minimum analysis on this whatsoever.

For instance, I have knowledge that in one major corporate acquisition many years ago that projected cost savings of combining two supply chains of the merging organizations was $XX,000,000 (specific number intentionally not included but it was eight figures). The savings required my approval and had to be supported by analysis. Eventually there was a proposal that included savings of both labor and materials, but do you know where it all started? … a number written on a sticky note after a five-minute meeting…. I am not criticizing the analysis that eventually was provided; however, the analytical process should come before the number.

For brevity, I'm shortening the list of human cost factors for personnel reductions with specific applicability to this discussion as follows:

1. Separation Costs

2. Replacement costs

3. Lost contacts and skill set

4. Decreased morale

5. Decreased productivity/increased inefficiencies

6. Increased absences

7. Increased needed training.

8. Increased litigation costs

9. Increased turnover

Money Not Motivational? It cannot be a complete discussion without mentioning Herzberg and his theories. I conducted extensive research on his theories a few years ago (2011) while researching retention issues, causes, and solutions. Essentially Herzberg said that money and extrinsic awards are not considered motivational factors, but they would qualify as dissatisfiers, and further, they do not significantly impact whether someone stays in their current job or leaves for another. This was concluded after Herzberg studied several companies and employees within 30 miles of Pittsburgh, Pennsylvania many decades ago (1950's and 1960's). It is now a set of conclusions in which many talent managers still base compensation decisions today. These conclusions are used despite the fact that this research was so small in scope and in working conditions that are very difficult to be found today. These few sentences comprise an extreme simplification of his writings and I encourage each of you to conduct your own research. Convincing you of a specific view on this topic is not the purpose. The purpose is to introduce you to information which you may not be routinely exposed, so you can have it for consideration as you make career choices.

No question that the pride of supporting the organization's mission is a factor in this discussion, as well as enjoying the people with whom you work. When you can join efforts with others to make something greater than you can do by yourself, there is a lot to be said for that, along with the satisfaction that goes with it. That is especially true if that mission is in support of the defense of this country, or in the defense of the environment, or some other worthy cause like in the medical field. Any time you are supporting a company to provide a product, it is because someone needs it. It may be an essential part of their (the customer's) life such as a medicine or food, or it may be something that makes their life better such as safety features or a new application for mobile devices. It is a great calling in life to be able to help others while on your job.

Similarly, recognition of individuals has been found to be beneficial to contributing to employee happiness. Having said that, current research and polls tend to disagree with Herzberg's conclusions. Both in 2010 (Towers Watson) and 2016 (Willis Towers Watson) global employee surveys showed that salary and benefits were the number one issue for both retention and attraction of employees. This is not a theory; this is what employees said. Money is number one to the worker community.

It was, however, not number one on the survey for employers. If employers do not understand or know what is important to employees, how can they effectively manage employees or efficiently produce whatever product or service they have. This brings into question management's ability to accomplish either.

This is a big disconnect. Obviously, that is a challenge that employers should resolve within themselves, because employees bring the products and solutions to the employers. It is their economy and decision to either stay on their job or seek work elsewhere. Whether employers believe this or not, employees have the power. Companies would be well served to ensure they have management that possesses multi-generational thought diversity to have winning ideas when it comes to recruitment.

If there are employers who will pay, there are employees who will go where they will be paid. It is supply and demand. It has nothing to do with raising the minimum wage or any other study or regulation. If there is a supply of higher paying jobs and there is a demand for higher paying jobs, people will go to them. The organizations who choose not to pay the money will lose employees.

Several years back, in the 1990s, the shipbuilding industry was losing skilled tradesmen in waves. Shipbuilders were hiring people from places like Vietnam and Central America to perform critical welding tasks due to the shortage, which surprised many. Visas were being extended, and many other things were being attempted to provide some type of band-aid solution. In a briefing I made to the Assistant Secretary of the Navy for Research, Development, and Acquisition, there were many factors across the industry nationwide contributing to why there was a shortage. But it really came down to one fact. The skilled tradesmen were leaving for higher pay, and the shipyards did not want to pay them. Therefore, the shipbuilders chose to lose the employees, even if it were over $.50/hour. It was that simple.

Who were the benefactors? Who got the labor? At that point in time the price of oil had gone up so there was a significant build up in the oil industry. To accomplish that build up in labor, oil related companies were paying more money. Also, the construction of casinos on the Gulf Coast were providing jobs for welders – as card dealers in the air conditioning. Welders in the South were exposed to extreme summer heat and they were able to get better paying jobs where they were not working with steel outside in 100-degree weather. When I am talking about more money, I am not talking about huge sums of money. In some cases, it was one or two dollars an hour with overtime. In other cases it was $.50/hour with overtime. The difference in many cases made it hard to understand why companies would not match or beat their competition pay-wise.

So again – the choice the shipbuilders made was to not pay... AND the consequences of their choice was extremely poor quality and workmanship. Anytime you go from a journeyman/apprentice ratio of

6:1 to 2:1, quality, schedule, and cost will all be impacted – negatively and in a big way.

The discussion would not be complete without that understanding because that will always be the result. "You get what you pay for" could never be a more apropos adage. When you lose experienced employees in any industry, quality will absolutely go down. That goes for yesterday, today – in 2018, and will be applicable every year after.

So what can an organization do to retain you? That is for you to decide, and that is why this discussion is included in this text. *Know Your Value and Act.* Briefly, though, there are some who put forth the theory that if you value your employees or potentially those with the greatest production value, why not pay them more than the market average? After all, it could be considered a long-term investment by securing their productive services. (Pink, 2009). If you are not aware that there is a potential divergence in theory, you may not be informed enough to know your value and to process all relevant information and make the best decision for your family, your mission, and "your" passion. Remember, it is your choice.

There are also still many in the workforce that do not understand just because you are doing a good job does not mean you will get a raise or a promotion. I have even seen one resume where the person literally wrote one sentence on his resume to cover a job he was working, and doing very well at it. I asked the first-line supervisor to ask that job applicant what was going on with his resume that he submitted. He may well have been the most qualified person for the promotion. The supervisor came back and said the employee told her that "we knew what he was doing and he didn't feel like he should have to write more". However, based on his submitted resume all I could do for him was shake my head in disbelief. Why would anyone intentionally sabotage their career, or at least their chances for promotion? That was an extremely arrogant and misguided act. The only real use for that resume at that point would be to recycle it in a horse stall. Of course, that was not done. But just sayin'....

There were other instances in my career where the person did not adequately describe current responsibilities or accomplishments on their resume. You have to take some personal responsibility throughout your career, and make good choices. Putting together a professionally acceptable application and resume package is one of them. No one will look out for you if you cannot perform the minimum amount of effort to perform due diligence. If you really want a job, go after it. Put in the proper time necessary to represent yourself and prepare yourself. That includes putting together a professional resume.

Don't Forget About Development. Another factor not previously discussed is development. This is the case where some organizations have more flexibility by offering great development opportunities without paying the preferred amount in salary. There is definitely a value associated with any type of development or training activity. You have to decide if it will give you long-term benefit, short-term benefit, or marginal benefit. Development and training have very real costs, with some classes or development being very expensive.

In those cases, development opportunities have to be weighed. Is this development you need in the next two years and to help you jumpstart your career? Is this development which will benefit you for your entire career? In those cases, you need to determine where it will take you job-wise (e.g. responsibility, geographic) and whether or not it will help you attain your salary level and benefits necessary to support your mission statement and your family unit.

In most of those instances there is a service period which has to be repaid in return for the leadership opportunity. It has been observed that many states, for example, pay for teachers' college expenses while in school, in return for a commitment of a period of time where the teachers go to an underserved geographic area. A lot of times these areas are very rural or have an economically depressed characterization. How does this match with your mission statement? If it takes you down a path where you have training with no parallel to your mission statement, it probably is not a wise move. Even if the development is targeted for a period of career in which you are not ready, you should probably decline that consideration. However, if you can leverage it for your desired career success, it could be just the thing to get you on a fast track with the added development and experience while helping those in great need.

Talk to Your Manager. If you really love where you work, but are still looking to get that extra edge, and feel like you are potentially experiencing career stagnation, ask your manager if there are unpublicized developmental programs. You never know until you ask. There could be something there. If they say no, you are in no worse a position and perhaps will even open up a dialogue with management where additional responsibilities for you are considered.

What Color is the Grass? So why is it you are going on the interview? The grass is not always greener. Today someone can look up an organization on Glassdoor and find out about the pay, the culture, and about the senior leader of an organization. It is a tremendous resource, and it is very insightful to have this information at your fingertips. Even then, there will be surprises because every organization is different.

If after this review it matches your mission statement and career goals, go for it. After all, - sometimes the grass is, in fact, greener....

Chapter 7

INTERVIEW TIP #2 – CONFIDENCE

You should have every confidence in the world that you are doing a good job. Doing your very best is what you owe your employer for the salary you are paid. It is a contract. You work; they pay.

Believe in yourself. That is just the basic premise of working, and after all everyone has a customer. If you do a good job you get repeat business and get to keep your job. However, a job does not have to be a lifelong or career-long servitude. This does not mean if you have the greatest job in the world and have growing responsibilities your entire career you could not work for one employer. It is possible, but highly unusual.

Communicate Please. You are free to apply for whatever job you desire at any given point. However, it is appropriate, and a responsibility, that you inform management. Communication is always critical in professional relationships. Should your manager get a call for a reference after your interview, you do not want them to be surprised. If they are surprised and act surprised to the person calling in, it sends a negative signal of poor communication on your behalf for both current and prospective management. It is worth noting that if the manager acts surprised because they are surprised, it is not their fault. It puts your prospects for the new job at risk, and risks damaging your relationship with your management on your current job. Again, this is basic employer-employee respect and courtesy. You are expected to know this on day 1.

I understand, though, that some reading this will not know this intuitively. I have seen examples in the workforce when the employee clearly did not understand it and did the opposite of what he or she should have done with basic communication. There are many who say that workers entering the workforce directly out of college are not ready for the culture shock of the corporate world. What is clear, though, is that everyone can improve in communication, and this is key to success on so many fronts.

Pushing is Allowed. If you have done your best, and have been there an acceptable period of time (that is up for a debate but I think at least a year, though it could be more) management should support you and want the best for you. In cases of internal jobs there could be an encouraging push from your current management to put in for another job at your current company if you have exhibited good work habits, know how to get along with others, and can accomplish wins. This has happened to me at least three times in my career. After I pursued through application and interviews, I got the job in each case. Be aware of those signals; watch for them. Do not miss them. Managers may be suggesting you put in for a job. Usually they are not just being nice and passing the time of day. It's a hint. Perhaps even a "hack". Your chances are probably good unless you bomb with a one-line representation on your resume. Still SMH. (still should have been put in a horse stall)

A funny side-story (but I did not think so at the time) is that on one of those suggestions from management I initially was not going to put in for the job. During this time I was working in New Orleans and I really liked the job, the people, my manager, the culture – everything about it, even though I was commuting 65 miles a day (one way). I know…. What was I thinking? 130 miles a day was just crazy. (Technically it was 131 miles but who is counting.) But there is just something about New Orleans that attracted me. There is so much more than just the French Quarter.

While the potential job was with a different part of the organization, it still had the same parent organization and I was a known factor and quantity based on my performance. The job was open for two weeks and week one was almost gone and the unthinkable occurred on the way home. I had a wreck. I was okay – a little sore. But the very next day, after a very quick reanalysis of the factors and a conversation with my wife, I put in for the job, and got it – and we moved again. It is amazing the events that trigger new steps along the career path. Don't miss out on the hints and "hacks" along the way.

Building Trust is Vital. If your best effort includes doing your job at a high level, getting along well with others, and doing everything you can to support the manager's mission and success, it is very rare when a manager does not support the person seeking to better their career (and family) status. It does not mean that the manager is happy about you leaving. But they realize that when you support them and their organizational mission, that it is a two-way street with trust. You have your personal mission and career you are supporting, and you need your manager to support you in return. Good managers understand this concept very well. You are not in servitude to them or to your current organization. You are essentially a borrowed asset and resource for a period of time. Many variables play into how long an organization gets to use you as a resource. Every time I have given a reference for an employee, the message has always been, the person "has always been a good employee, - and I don't know what I will do without (him or her)"! Each time the employee received an offer.

Have the confidence to move forward with your career. Take hold of it. No one is going to take care of you professionally – or your family - better than you. Absolutely no one! While it does not mean that managers do not care for you - your mission, your career, your job, your family – is your choice.

Chapter 8

INTERVIEW TIP #3 –
TELL YOUR STORY

Everyone has a story - a story of success and a story of accomplishments. You need to know your story going into the interview. It is your ticket to success and your career future. Know your top five accomplishments you want interviewers to know, and always have a silver bullet at the end for "is there anything you would like to add" or "do you have any questions? That question will come. It will come at the end.

Know and Tell Your Story. If you are timed (e.g. 30 minutes) and you have five questions, plan out the structure of the interview. Don't mistakenly think that is six minutes per question (30/5). You will leave no time for your silver bullet. Also, if they provide you a written list of the questions, politely decline the interviewers reading the questions if they offer. That is your time they are wasting, and certainly you can read them silently to yourself and save time. However, if there is no option you still want to wisely use your time. Be aware of the time element. You must tell "Your Story". That is your ticket.

No matter what you are asked, tailor "Your Story" to the questions. You will always be asked about working in a team, and working cordially with others. Demonstrated initiative is also likely to be questioned in some way. Most likely you will also be asked what you would do in some type of defined or undefined work crisis. Tell "Your Story". It is

"Your Story" that will sell; it is "Your Story" that you have confidence in. It is "Your Story" that makes you different from the other candidates. Tell it. Do not read it – Tell it! If you cannot sell "Your Story", why would anyone buy it?

But Don't…. On topic, let me explain a couple of things you should not do in interviews. These actually happened, so I did not make these up – though I am very sure some of you reading this will be ready to wager that these two stories are total fabrications.

The first example was in an instance where the job was a mid-level type job and interviews were being conducted after resume submission. The question was asking the candidate to describe any weaknesses they may have. The reply back was, "I eat too much." Even though the answer which was supplied to us was **obviously true** (visual observation), his answer to the question should have been professionally related. So do not mistakenly start talking about personal or family issues relating to any of the job-related questions you will be asked. That person was obviously not prepared for his interview or taking his job search very seriously.

Another example of what not to do for an interview was related to another mid-level job interview I conducted. The person was supposed to be at their phone at a certain coordinated time for a phone interview since they were out of town. Well the person was called at the appointed time, and there was no answer. Voicemail kicked on. After about 10 minutes of trying, the person finally answered their phone. The first thing this lady said, after we, as panel members, introduced ourselves to her was, "Is this going to take long?" My response to her was, "No. Not at all." Sure enough it did not take much time at all to quickly ask the questions and to receive her answers. That was obviously the last time she heard from us. Do not act as if the interview panel is inconveniencing you. You have worked for this, and now is your time to shine.

In summary, the three tips for interviews are-

Why?

Confidence

Tell Your Story

PART 3

GETTING READY FOR YOUR JOB

Chapter 9

LEADERSHIP MARKETING

Personal branding is something where you can have a single phrase or a few words that captures what type of professional you are or what type of product you produce. This is not meant to be a purpose statement, career goals, or a mission statement per se. It is short, and conveys concisely that brand. For instance, my brand is I am a customer solution designer. I can strip back all of the technical and management skills, certifications, training, and experience to the very core of what I do. Companies and individuals have brands, whether they want them or not.

You Are Branded. What is your personal brand? Do you consistently provide high quality products on time and every time? Those characteristics sound like a brand would be easy to describe. I think a brand of "Provider of On Time Products" would be a good choice. What about an engineer who has time and again come up with innovative and new techniques with two patents pending? I think a brand of "Leading Edge Engineering Innovator" would be a good personal brand for such a person. You may have other ideas, and that is certainly okay. There is no right or wrong, but it is important to know how this affects your career.

It is Leadership Marketing. Everything the Engineer does professionally would support that brand, but the continual process of providing and marketing ideas in meetings, briefings, conferences and everyday activities is more of a holistic application of marketing concepts. It would be called Leadership Marketing.

Leadership Marketing is so much more than branding. This encompasses nearly every interaction in which you engage. It does not matter if the communication is remote or in person, you are exchanging ideas. The degree to which you provide information and ideas is what I call Leadership Marketing.

It is said that everyone can be a leader. Not everyone believes that. Some believe that you are born a leader. This view somehow superimposes a genetic background as key to being a leader. Human study has not supported that presumptive conclusion.

Choosing to Put In Effort to Be a Leader. Based on personal experience and observation, I believe that should you choose to be a leader and put in the time, training, determination, and effort to be a leader, you can be a leader. I have seen; however, people desire to be a leader, but are unwilling to do what is necessary to reach that end. Consequently, they will never be a leader.

As an example, I implemented Speed Coaching for professionals in one of my former career assignments. It was designed to get the employee requesting the coaching to look very hard at their career plan, and at least have a career plan in writing. The good thing about the effort was that approximately 60% of the participants had either written or had committed to write a career plan, as a result of the coaching. My cutoff to determine if the event was successful was a stated 50% goal. If a singular event can result in positive behavioral influence or change in over half the participants, that is a great return on investment.

While the questions were scripted to the very limited time allocation per person, there was one person's interaction I recall vividly (as I also volunteered to be a coach for the event). When this coachee was asked why he wanted to be a supervisor and a leader, I felt like (perception and paraphrase) the response was, "well I think I will do pretty good at it. I think that is what is expected and that is what I want to do. I think I can get along with people."

I do not remember the exact words. But the prior feedback I had received, personal knowledge of the person and his delivery of intent, did not match up with the intent of really wanting to be a supervisor and leader. His words actually matched with the preconceived notion. His conveyance was really that he was not ready and he did not want to put in the time to get ready. That does not mean that he could not change. It is a choice. In a world, though, where perception is reality, that person did not do well with his leadership marketing. People are born to choose – everything in life, and being a leader is one thing that has to be chosen. It is not something with which you are born.

Back to Leadership Marketing - When you are giving advice to your child, in addition to good parenting that could also be considered as leadership marketing. The relationship is totally different from a professional relationship; you can pretty much tell a kid what to do. But that is not always the best way to go about things. Most of the time it is better when you can talk with your child and teach them why you want them to do something or not do something. Those are precious learning moments that have a good chance of sticking with them. Obviously, there are multiple paths that can go. When they are one or two years old it may not be the best opportunity to have philosophical conversations. But later, a good conversation where the real learning point is conveyed can have a better down-road impact. (not intended as parental advice.... the real point is illustrating or demonstrating how discussing a topic in a certain way can amplify the understanding level. This is audience and experience specific.)

At work when you are in a meeting and your participation is required, whatever you contribute is a form of leadership marketing. Frankly, should you not participate while attending a meeting, that, also, is leadership marketing and a snapshot of you. As an example, there was a series of meetings a few years ago in which I was a principal dealing with certain issues. As part of the meetings the other organization's senior executive would start reading his mobile device when the topic turned to an angle of the topic in which he either did not support or did not understand. His leadership marketing efforts were screaming that he was extremely rude and arrogant, among other things. It made a lasting impression on everyone there. Similarly, your contributions in the meetings you support will send out leadership marketing messaging. By the way, a few months later this executive's behavior in front of other executives led to his retirement in a timeframe much sooner than he had planned!

Another good example of leadership marketing would be when you are meeting with your manager over office issues. Whatever comments or issues or work products you talk about, your side of the meeting will be in the form of leadership marketing.

An example of a public company getting involved in leadership marketing to support a brand is Proctor and Gamble. In 2007 and 2008, they came out with an ad campaign focusing on the Tide Spot Remover. They integrated their "family friendly products" brand in this. They did this by focusing on a product. They followed this up with a campaign of "Thank You Mom" in support of the Olympics in 2010. They carried that ad campaign for a few years. The brand was "family friendly products". In this push they focused on the brand itself. In both of those cases, and in other public interactions they were conducting leadership marketing to establish and solidify their brand with the obvious hopes of increasing sales.

Being aware that every interaction you have is you personally marketing to someone else is a different way to think about your communications with others. There is no escaping, the person who masters leadership marketing will be successful with either formal or informal authority. The reason for that is they are obviously communicating to share their ideas, positions, and thoughts. Focus on leadership marketing will make the individual and business unit stronger. No matter how hard or how little you try, you use leadership marketing every day. You should then choose to use it to your advantage. Keep that in mind as we proceed into the next chapters will discuss the principles of 3.6 Leadership.

PART 4

3.6 LEADERSHIP

Chapter 10

3.6 LEADERSHIP POINT #1 - ACTION

When you arrive on your job you want to do everything you can to find out what your exact assignments are and where you fit into the organization and its mission, so you can actively and proactively produce your service for your manager and the organization. As such, Action, is the first element of 3.6 Leadership.

While your manager should play a prominent role in discussing expectations, giving you the tools to be successful, and laying out training requirements for you in order to have the immediate hands-on short-cuts related to organizational and system-wide expectations, do not be surprised if that does not happen. Sometimes the employee gets the short end of the stick in order for mission focus to be the priority. Should it not happen there are options available to you.

Just Do It. Ideally there will be a person in the work group tagged with being your eyes and ears to help you through these processes. If that is not evident, it would show the supervisor your initiative if you asked him or her for such a point person. Chances are your supervisor has a very heavy workload and they may not have had a chance to prepare adequately for your arrival. That is not an excuse, but is an opening for you to get on the supervisor's good side as this would show you are already focused on providing action necessary to help that supervisor to be successful. Really their bottom-line for you is to make you productive as soon as possible. So this would serve as a win/ win for both you and your supervisor.

Get a copy of the organization's mission statement if one is not already in your possession. While that is not going to tell you what your specific responsibility is, it starts to lay out the corner pieces of the puzzle. With that, you can then ask your supervisor what his or her top three overall concerns are in his or her job, and how that may translate into his or her top three challenges for you.

If you have already been in your job for a period of time (this could be anytime over a couple of months), you can ask for a meeting with your supervisor to hit the reset button and potentially gain a new and improved dialogue with the supervisor. This can happen even if you are on good speaking terms and believe you have a good relationship. It could start in the meeting like this. "I know we have been very busy lately, but I wanted to talk to you a little more on current challenges. I would like to ask you what your overall top three challenges are, and what your top three priorities for me are." This can be reworded 100 different ways. The point is it is an opportunity for you to connect – today – in a meaningful way, and in a way that can show you how to make your manager successful. There has never been a meeting with the manager like that where the manager was not happier at the end of the meeting. All managers want to be successful. If they see their people trying to make them successful – well – that is a good thing!

Additionally, be proactive to join teams and to get to know people. This goes if you are in the job on day 22 or year 22. It is never too late to be a part of a team and join in for a team success. Chances are you will be asked to work on teams to accomplish unit success, but there could be opportunities to participate on organizational efforts or initiatives. It is those teams that contribute to strategic planning or another initiative such as organizational events which are also important to culture and state of mind. Making relationships outside of your unit is always a good thing. As I have said in another place in this book, you can never have too many friends or contacts. What if you are asked to lead an effort in your unit involving best practices of a process. If you know one of your fellow team members at the organizational level has a practice with a lot of success, guess what? Your contact can get you a great jump start on your assignment.

Always show initiative and action in your career. If you are invested in your personal mission statement, you should invest with initiative in the organization where you are.

Chapter 11

3.6 LEADERSHIP POINT #2 - ATTITUDE

There is no disputing that relationships based on trust go a long way in determining if you will be viewed as a positive or negative influence in your work environment. You should do everything positive in getting off on the right foot. It is all about attitude.

Find out who the key players are in your organization. There are those who have formal authority such as your management chain. But there are also those who have authority based on experience, knowledge, and sometime based solely on personality. In many instances this informal authority comes from a combination of both. By learning this you will understand the important centers of power in your organization.

Get To Know People. Everyone has strengths. They may not be evident at first, but try to find out at least one thing about those with whom you work. During your first few days, the single thing may not be necessarily a positive thing. But do not let that discourage you from trying to get to know people and to find that strength. Your attempts to be friendly and to fit in as a positive team member will be looked at favorably by most. They will see you as having a "good" attitude. As a memory aid, once or twice a day try to write these things you find out about your co-workers or managers in a notebook just for reference purposes. This will help you as you get up to speed and start working with these people in your new job. You will have this record of notes to read on people when you find out you will be either working with them or for them in some capacity.

Be aware though, that some people do not like change. They may wear these feelings outwardly "on their sleeves". That means, they want to drive on the same road to work, enter in the same door, sit in the same office cube, and work with the same people. They do not want a new manager, new responsibility, or a new co-worker. Do not take it personal should you be slighted with this type of worker. It does not mean you should totally ignore them. When you are required to work with them be as cordial as you can to them. You never know what a person's backstory is.

Don't Give Up on People. Sometimes people have so much baggage in their personal life that they only want things with absolutely no change during work hours. You never know what someone is going through. Factually speaking, everyone has something on their personal plate that may be challenging. It could be a sick child, an elderly parent with whom they have to watch and literally have to take care of by themselves, or their adult child may have burned out in college or after college. You just never know. That is not an open door to be a psychologist (unless that is your job and they are a paying patient). But be aware, and understanding. Again, try not to take things personally.

Customer Relationships. A positive relationship with customers is a major area in your job regardless of what your job is. Everyone has a customer. They can be more traditional (i.e. external customers), or they can be internal customers. Sometimes we lose sight of who our customer is – even at the organization level. However, it is those relationships with customers that are so key.

Often, it takes extra efforts to establish relationships with customers. Try to understand their perspective. They will always have pressures and demands to meet schedules. What can you do to help them? What can you do to make their job easier? It will help you do your job, if you help them do their job. These relationships are essential. This is an area that should be on your list to talk about with your manager. He or she will be most interested in customer relationships because there is a direct linkage to customer satisfaction. If your customers are happy, that goes a long way in keeping management happy and is a symbol of meeting mission. Be aware, though, if you fail with your relationships with your customers, you will fail in your job. That is just a fact.

Suppliers are Also Key. Having positive attitudes with suppliers is also an area that sometimes get overlooked. In many instances, you may have internal suppliers you depend on. An example is that doctors and nurses in hospitals depend on the hospital pharmacy to provide critical medicines in a timely manner to treat patients and their symptoms. If a patient is very sick or in great pain, it could stress the front-line healthcare (i.e. nurses) giver to get the medicine immediately. In some instances, nurses are waiting on the doctors to write the prescription before sending it to a pharmacy. What would happen if the nurse started yelling at the pharmacy staff because the medicine was not delivered on time? What would happen if the nurse started yelling at the doctor? Obviously, nothing good would happen if anyone started yelling. A lot of trust would be broken, the person being yelled out will not be as eager to help the nurse with the request. Who really gets hurt in this case? The patient. Always try to understand what the end-game consequence is of any relationship or action.

You can see from this simple illustration that we need things from others in our organization. What if you have an organization which needs legal review of a document before you proceed. Should you just wait until the document is one week overdue before you check? There are so many easy ways to politely follow up with suppliers, internal or external, and still find out the status.

For instance, what if you called the internal supplier and asked, "I just wanted to call to see how things were going? The concept was very challenging for me and I wanted to see if there was anything that I could try to explain while you are reviewing the document." How innocuous is that? No one gets offended or excited, and there actually could be a point or two of clarification that is needed. So, three things happened in that exchange. First, you found out the status. Second, the supplier found out you were nice to talk to, and if a problem does come up in review then would feel comfortable in calling you back. That may save time along the process. Third, if there is a problem, you were successful in expediting it with the supplier by the exchange of information.

That can be tailored for any supplier, internal or external. What happens if you have not been dealing with your suppliers like this before now, and you do not have a good relationship with them? There is always a starting place.

Burning a Bridge. Never burn a bridge. Nothing good ever comes of that. An example is there was one organization I had worked for very early in my career, and had gotten along great with my management. There was an issue with one of the managers after I left. The manager had a reserved parking spot next to the building. As the story goes, there was a person working in the same overarching organization who decided they would park in his parking spot one day. This manager did not like it to say the least. While he found out who the rule breaker was, he decided he was going to pen a tersely worded note for the perpetrator and leave on his vehicle instead of handling it more diplomatically. I have no knowledge of what the note said, but I am pretty sure it did not say, "Will you be my friend?"

The next day that same person parked in his parking spot again. The story I heard was the manager was fuming but did not write another note. The last piece of the story told to me was that at the end of the day, apparently, the perpetrator had four flat tires. The manager reportedly had put tiny rocks in the tire stems in each of the tires and screwed the caps tightly on the tire stems. Wow! That is where the fact-pattern ended. Oh… no one ever parked in his parking place again.

What was the end in mind the manager wanted to accomplish? He did not want anyone to park in his space again. Well he accomplished that. But what about viewing that person and that person's office as a supplier. What kind of effort do you think was given if that manager or his office needed support from the perpetrator's office? I am not suggesting the perpetrator was right. But there was most certainly a better way of addressing the issue rather than flatting all four tires. What are you really wanting to accomplish?

Building relationships in your organization, as well as with customer and suppliers are key to being successful in any office, and it absolutely in no way has anything to do with your grade, rank, status, or any other characteristic that would make you believe that it does not apply to you. No exceptions.

Chapter 12

3.6 LEADERSHIP POINT #3 - AWARENESS

When you first arrive on your job, or if you have been in your job a while, it is never too late to make a difference. In Chapter 9, I talked about trying to find out what the mission is and trying to understand how you fit in. That is very key. This is also a great time to try to analyze how your personal mission statement links to the organizational mission.

At this point you have already made your decision that you are in the right job at the right time. But it may not have been clear whether or not the organizational mission matches your personal mission. There are three reasons why you would not know.

1. You are new to the job and even though you knew the mission's words, you did not know what they meant as defined by your current management.

2. You have been in the job for a while, and frankly, management has not placed a priority on strategic goals or missions, and so it is an out of sight type thing.

3. You have been in the job for a while, and now management is placing a priority on all things strategic.

In any of these three instances it is important for you to understand what is driving the organization. The mission is usually the compass. But it may be possible that the mission is only being paid lip-service. Even in that case something is driving the organization. Has it become a reactionary organization to directives from corporate HQ? There can be several scenarios, but how you play in this organization's direction gives you important information on what your true role is.

Finding the Compass. The vision of the organization is more of a view of what the organization is desiring to accomplish. Contrasted, the mission pertains to the objective and factual statement of what the organization accomplishes with its product or services. The strategic plan is a roadmap that allows the accomplishment of the mission and will hopefully allow for the completion of the vision.

This is another key indicator of the organization. Where does the organization want to go? The vision will let you know. If the organization has no vision, well – I have no comment other than that is concerning. That would be a statement about the current leadership. (Well, that probably does fit the mold of a comment….)

Usually the mission is clear, but the vision ignites passion. That is why I call it passion instead of vision. It is this passion that gives you a snapshot of the future. Does your personal mission statement fit with the organization's vision? If that is not obviously clear, try to get plugged into the strategic planning extension of the organization if possible. Most likely, larger organizations will have a need to include employees to assist in the planning process. Smaller organizations may tend to keep that more close hold in the planning stages. Execution is everyone's ballgame. Therefore, you will be directly responsible for the execution of your part of the strategic plan. Even though it is probably down to the goal level, and potentially even in the business plan goal of it (business plan is short-term and usually one year only), your efforts and action are responsible for the success of the organization. When you have specific accomplishments supporting the execution of the organization's mission, strategic and business plans, you need to capture that as a "so what". Remember our prior discussion on resumes?

What really is next? Is it clear from the strategic plan? Is it clear from the vision? Or perhaps there are new management initiatives from corporate headquarters on what seems to be a continuous basis? That happens on occasion. That is not efficient as the organization has no time to gain synergy from getting lean or process improvement programs to reap "best of" practices or to eliminate wasteful steps. As a matter of principle these continual changes from corporate, if that is the case, keep moving the mark and it makes efficiencies not possible because it continues to change the baseline.

Knowing what is next is sometimes tough to know. Often a great relationship with your manager can help you identify future organizational changes better than other alternatives.

Beware of gossip and those that gossip. Usually that is never a good thing and is usually never good information. Those that gossip are weak-minded and prey on those who are like them.

Stay focused on what is important.

Chapter 13

3.6 LEADERSHIP POINT #4 - ATTRACTION OF NEW IDEAS

New ideas are the life blood of an organization. It has been accurately said that an organization is either growing or it is dying. It grows with new personnel, strategies, and with new ideas. New ideas do not have to necessarily come with new people, but that is what you hope to get when you get new workers in the organization. Fresh ideas.

How can you tell if an organization is one that supports innovation? One can look at the mission and vision and strategic plan and get an indication as to whether or not it at least makes it to paper. That does not mean that it is really taken seriously by the organization. Too often we hear, "that's the way we have always done it". My only thought and reply to that is, "that's interesting", or "noted".

Employees Know. Frankly, if that is the organization's overarching approach, it does not stop you from identifying better ways of accomplishing something. All real literature of both process improvement and lean will tell you, it is not management who makes change. It is not management who even knows the processes. If you ask management what they believe the processes are, they will most certainly give you an answer. But that answer will correlate to how things have always been done, or how things should be done in their view. They do not know what is actually going on at the detail level. If there is a manager who states they are different, they are sorely misguided or they just came off the floor in the last month to become a manager. That is my opinion based on significant amounts of research in process improvement, lean, and activity based costing. Moreover, with years of experience in management that was always the case, personally.

By extension, the ones who can make the difference and who can make the change are at the worker levels. You can make a difference. If you are new to management, or are in first-line management, you are the exception in that you may know most of the process as compared to other managers. Because an efficient management platform does not have a manager review everything, it still will be the worker who knows the process the best.

Again, a worker can always work with other owners of the process to make things better. Who does not want a faster process that has less steps and takes less time? The reason that many of these great ideas are never revealed is that at some point a great idea was shunned by a co-worker or manager, and the source of that idea has given up on innovation. You can make a difference in innovation. You can start something with initiative and desire. If you are a manager, you can give your staff space to work, space to create, space to invent. Sometimes all it takes is a "yes", or "give it a shot".

Poor Communication Costs Money. Illustrating this by a personal example, the first week I became a manager, my second level manager came in my office at 1:50 PM one day and asked me what I was doing. I then replied back, "what would you like for me to do?" Not real intuitive – but you should realize when someone is asking you something besides the actual words stated. He said there was an Integrated Product Team (IPT) meeting that started in 10 minutes. I said no problem and that I will cover. He added, "There is one more thing. You are running the meeting." LOL. Not sure what exactly I said but it was something probably with a laugh and an "I got it".

The meeting was just short of an all-out brawl inside of five minutes into the meeting. The meeting was with our prime multi-billion-dollar contractor and the contracting process had fallen into a hole, and there was no meaningful relationship in place. Times were taking way too long, mission was being impacted, and our customer was very displeased. Additionally, the extra process time was costing real money as construction was ongoing. Later changes meant rip-out of existing construction, essentially meaning the ripped-out work was costing to rip-out. This resulted in the initial construction of the desired change area to be a sunk cost with no return. I wound up having to break up the meeting early as there were no agreements on anything, and everyone disputed the perception and opinions of the other side. It was just a "rudefest"!

A New Way. A very long story made moderately short was the next meeting I was prepared. We set up ground rules such as no cussing, throwing things, no personal attacks - just basic courtesy – and one more thing – no arguing about perceptions. Perceptions were reality and we had to work things out down to that level. After a few weeks of intense cooperation and two-way communication, which had never been previously utilized, the entire process was reworked. Essentially the old process was thrown out completely with a new process taking its place. Result was contract actions took 60% less time. That is time and money saved. This was lean before lean became in vogue.

Just Say Yes. As a result of that innovative success, I was asked to take over the strategic planning for my organization; they had never had a strategic plan. I could have said no. But I said yes.

Sometimes all it takes is a "yes" and the risk of trying something new. I have had innovative successes throughout my career, and have enabled those who have worked for me to innovate and create new paths, processes, and systems if they dared to say yes. That is something that every one of you can do. It does not matter what job, what company, and what level your job is. You can bring innovation and make a difference - by just saying yes. Do not be afraid of taking a risk.

Chapter 14

3.6 LEADERSHIP POINT #5 - COMMUNICATION

In one office where I was a manager and had been in the job only a couple of months, I had a team leader knock on my door asking to talk with me. She said what she had to say was going to make me mad, but she needed to tell me any way. As I recall I sat back not really knowing what to expect. Did someone get hurt, quit, make a customer mad or steal money? After all, if this report was going to make me mad I wanted to be ready for the worst.

She went on to explain an issue where a procedure was not followed, or something occurred where the process was broken, and it resulted in a non-positive conclusion. She eventually finished her story and there was a pause. I asked her if there was anything else, and she replied, "No. Aren't you mad?" I cannot even remember what it was that she reported to me.

I explained I was not mad, and that what she did was exactly what I hoped she would do, and what everyone else working for me would do - just let me know truthfully what has occurred. We could then work first, on fixing the current problem. Later, we could then work on trying to prevent it in the future. Telling information like it is will be the key to communication and creating a culture of communication.

Communicate Problem and Solutions. I realize there may be managers that get upset when you give them complete information on problems. The only recommendation here for that and in any case, you need to disclose the full information as soon as you can, but always have at least two alternatives for solutions to give the manager when you bring the bad news. That way – you are not only bringing them a problem – but you are also giving them the solution to the problem. Do not just bring a problem. By bringing them two alternatives, then they can weigh in on the final mitigative action taken. You will find that there is a significant value assessment placed on you and other employees who can also bring solution alternatives with them. Being able to provide solutions will make you invaluable to your manager and organization. You will become known as either a problem solver or a solution creator.

Relationships with Customers. The most difficult thing you will ever do, though, is to establish and maintain an effective relationship with your customer. It does not matter how many zeros you put on the business line. It does not matter how many corporate officers you have to brief or manage. It does not matter if you have to brief the CEO or the President. It is your relationship with your customer that is most important. It will determine your success at every stop of your career.

Your customers are coming to you because they need your help. Chances are your customers speak a different language from you. I am not talking about the difference between Spanish, Chinese, or English. I am talking about what they are good at. It is, in fact, the thing that drives their passion. Therefore, they will speak the detailed language of their project, program, or their goal. This is a language you will need to learn to best meet their needs or requirements.

Let's go back to the hospital setting example we were using earlier. Now let's add another party to the scenario – the information technology office. The nurses, pharmacists, and doctors have enough medical training where they can pretty much speak a similar language – at least as far as prescribed drugs and impacts are concerned. Their capacities and focus are different, but they understand each other. What if the IT system is having problems transferring data real-time from the doctor stations to the hospital pharmacy? There is something the doctors are either being required to do that is an extra step, or the way it is being entered into the system, that is not being assimilated by the latest IT system upgrade. Something is wrong, and they cannot get the medicines they need for the treatment and well-being of their patients due to a system problem.

It is causing, in some cases, the manual delivery of the prescription by doctor's nurse practitioners to the pharmacy. That is critical time away from patient care that the doctor, nursing team, and patients cannot withstand. Now the doctor, the charge nurse, the nurse practitioner are all calling IT to fix the problem. The real issue is IT does not understand from the medical team what they are doing to trigger the problem, and they cannot relate to the urgency. If they did, they would have the issue fixed immediately as it would assume top priority status. The lack of common language is a real problem.

How many times do you think IT has walked a Round with the doctor team or spent a shift with the nurses to see how the systems are used? Zero? How many times have you asked your customer if you could visit their spaces, or their lab, or their design room, or in their production facility or to a product testing? (*crickets chirping in the woods….*) In many cases, I suspect the answer is also zero.

Maybe this is something you have already independently figured out. That is great! You have already discovered this linkage. The maintenance of that relationship is key. Keep working on it and making it better.

It is those visits to the customer that will gain the trust from them so they can speak your language, and you their language. You will help them to help you. In the world of contracts, if you are in the contract office and cannot get the customer to speak to you and provide a requirement in understandable language for you to put on a contract solicitation, your likelihood for success is also zero. It will not happen. You may swerve into it after several misfires. But the barrier has to be broken and the only way is through effective communication.

Earning Trust. How do you gain trust from your customer? That is easy to understand. If the customer is so smart on their product, their language on that product is naturally going to be over your head to some extent. If you give just a little more effort to establish that relationship, you will be absolutely amazed at the result. They will do everything they can do so you can understand them and their needs. Customers are people; just like people with whom you work beside in your office, or with whom you go to church. Do they have kids? Are they from out of state? Do they travel much? How is that relevant to your work product? In an isolated vacuum, there is not much correlation at all. However, if you are trying to establish a relationship, and a relationship is critical, it is directly related.

Survey Customers. On another directly related note. If you have a customer with a continual requirement, the following can be used as a customer survey. It is most effective, and it is the best customer survey I have seen or used. It contains two questions and administered verbally quarterly. I designed it with one thing in mind – your customer relationship will drive the level of your success. You should be talking with your customer much more than this, but quarterly is a sufficient time period for customer service assessment.

1. Overall, how would you rate the service that you have been provided in the last three months?

2. How would you rate the communication that you have been provided in the last three months?

That is all there is to it. You could have pen and paper handy to write. But rarely will it evolve into a long list of issues. This is a verbal survey given in a conversational style setting. Your customer wants to tell you this information, but rarely gives it in a useful manner without this open invitation. After your meeting with your customer, you should capture it on a 4-point scale.

The results are only as good as your honesty. If you record a 4 every time for both of these factors, and there are problems, what have you gained? Nothing except making yourself look like a fool, and wasting your customer's time and potentially trust. After all, if you are asking your customer how things are going and they give constructive feedback and you do not act on the feedback, how will it make them feel? The answer to that last question is most likely they will question your motives at best, but most likely it will anger them. What a customer says to you, especially in the context of a "really, how's it going" meeting, is vitally important. Those are the golden nuggets – the "gift" as one of my senior leaders taught me one time. This eye to eye contact and conversation is where you can really find out the key to where your relationship with the customer is.

You can have a challenging score on question one of the survey, but have a good score on question two, which is communication. You may also have a good score on both one and two. However, if you have a challenging score on two, your score on question one will also be lacking. You cannot be successful without having effective communication avenues and practices. If you have problems in communication, it absolutely will affect overall service. This turns into a very instructive graph over time for use by your team.

I said it was the best I ever used, and I did design it after gaining less than acceptable information or feedback from the longer surveys that no one has the time to answer. The second best survey ever was by the Geek Squad; it was a three-question survey. The longer these surveys are, the less meaning they have. I have also seen a one question survey used by Shopify. It is very easy to complete; it is just a little too high level from which to draw a lot of discernment. The question focuses on the overall experience and does not ask about communication.

People get tired of surveys and at a certain point they either delete them if they are online, or just put the same number or answer down for questions 6-15 without reading the questions. In that latter case, obviously the answers have little or no relevance.

The summary on customers is communicate or fail. It is that simple.

What About Employees? The last group you need to focus on with communication would be with employees. I talked a lot about building relationships with employees in Chapter 9. But it goes without saying, you cannot build relationships without communication. Often communication is filtered because people do not listen. Other times communication is filtered by personal biases or paradigms.

When I worked in New Orleans it was a big dose of a new type of culture for me. I really liked it. Not only is there an intriguing dialect, sometimes native New Orleanians had language phrases that were new to me. The easiest one to write about is when someone asks you "Where y'at?" It sounds very much like a condensed version of "Where are you at?" The first time I was asked that I was heading down the stairs and one of my counterparts with whom I had developed a friendship was going up the stairs. I replied, "Right here. Where are you at?" LOL. What they are really saying is "How are you doing?" I had no idea. That was not my paradigm. ...and we did laugh about that for several weeks and months.... Another one is "going to make groceries." "I'm going to make groceries", I would hear. You can look that one up if interested....

Another challenge for me is to always understand what people at the drive-thru line for a restaurant are saying through their speaker. Sometimes they may as well be talking Latin (I took Latin but I do not speak it – nor does anyone else; hence the analogy). So here the workers are talking Latin as I am trying to place an order. I know they cannot help it. They have no idea what they sound like or that they are talking Latin. Their view is probably that most people going in the drive-thru line are deaf. Some drive-thru lines now have the results of your order by the speaker. That is a help. That way you can quickly assess if your order was received correctly. But other times, without that electronic aid to verify the order, I grow weary of saying "what?" and just go to pick up my food surprise de jour.

Differences Make Us Stronger. Similarly, in today's world wherever you work, there will be people that are different from you. ...different skin pigment, accents, national origin or state origin, religion, single or married, political party, and the list goes on and on. If you have one kid and the person next to you in the office has six kids, you have no idea what the family of eight is going through. That is just life. Always remember the differences in people. Ask people questions to allow them to tell you what they want you to know. I am not talking about bothering people, but just appearing interested with the hopes of making a good working relationship. You can also share special things about yourself to assist the bonding process.

Differences are what make us unique, and differences are what make us strong. While often you will never get that from listening to TV news, check it out the next time you are in a group of five to seven people. There is a reason each of you has been invited. (I know sometimes you get "voluntold".) Still – you each have a strength in something. Try to listen or watch for it.

Having a culture of communication in an office is a great thing. You can do your part to contribute. Communicating is the absolute best way to garner success in your current job assignment, and is the key to accomplishing the other four factors in 3.6 Leadership.

PART 5

AVOID THE MAZE

Chapter 15

TOXIC TRAP #1 – TOXIC LEADERS

It seems at every Halloween, there are farms that enjoy setting up a maze in their fields. For a couple of dollars, people can come out and use their directional abilities to find their way out. Along the way there will be a couple of dead ends, and they will have to go in another direction. If you have ever tried a maze, it is a lot of fun even if you have to deal with dead ends. You deal with it, assess it, and move on. Similarly, from time to time there are some dead ends in some organizations that you have to deal with along the experience of your career. The first Toxic Trap discussed is that of toxic leaders.

Toxic leaders are found in most organizations. Why is that? Far too often leaders are formally chosen due to the fact that they have a technical skillset that is superior to their peers. They have excelled in solving problems or producing services or items when others could not get the job done. Therefore, they are put in charge of shaping, molding, and developing others to emulate them. This is not to imply that every leader in every organization is toxic or incapable of managing, or that most leaders are toxic. The point is that they are found everywhere.

There is a big problem with only selecting someone because they perform at a very high level technical level. Just because one possesses superior technical skills does not mean that they have either the training or the aptitude to manage other people. In virtually all cases of a toxic leader, one or both of those key factors are missing.

Know in 5 seconds. By extension, this type of leader has no clue there is a culture problem in his or her organization. They are blind to it. They keep their head down and do what they have always done - that is perform technical tasks. They have no idea how to manage or supervise people. They don't delegate; they don't communicate; and they expect their "subjects" to act and perform exactly like them without any guidance. In a compelling article in LinkedIn, John Eades (2017, January 10) writes that leaders should first acknowledge if a problem exists. "Plenty of cultural assessments exist on the market, but the simplest test is to ask yourself, 'Do my people like coming to work'? You should be able to answer this question in less than 5 seconds. If you falter, you might have a culture problem." Toxic leaders always fail to acknowledge there is either a cultural issue or that it is their fault. But the five second rule is a good one to keep in mind.

For purposes of this discussion those toxic leaders are combined into one of three groupings.

1. They tell you what to think, how to do it and when. Since this type of toxic leader has superior technical skills, they believe those now working for him or her should exhibit the exact same skills and strengths and solve problems in the exact same way.

Mr. or Ms. Micro. For example, if those leaders solve a problem by individually working complex analytical statistical calculations, then they frown on those who work in teams to accomplish the same thing but in a totally different way. It does not matter to them that the person being assigned to solve the next set of challenging problems has very strong communication skills and probably has more leadership skills due to his or her communication abilities. It does not matter that they can build a coalition, consensus, and can ensure that both customers and suppliers are on the same page. Things are approached differently and are, therefore, unacceptable. You must do it their way and do it in the exact amount of time it took them to accomplish such a task – no exceptions. That is the way they have always done things.

2. They are king makers, not leaders or developers. This type of toxic leader is even more dangerous to the welfare of employees who work for them and the organizations in which they are charged to run.

Mr. or Ms. Politico. These leaders are not interested in managing people or developing people at all. They are interested in it for themselves. They like to make themselves look good and are willing to play politics and sacrifice any who get in their way. They will also tend to identify one or two people to hold onto their coattails in the process. The rationale behind that is not necessarily to help those people, but they have some attribute that can be useful to the leader as they try to work their way to a better position.

I have been extremely blessed to have so many great leaders in my career. They have been from all walks of life, race and gender. I have learned greatly from the strengths of each, and developed lifetime friendships with all of them. The common characteristic of each – they all cared about their people and could communicate it. Moreover, they supported the mission of the organization and were not involved in the immoral games played with personal gain and politics.

As a result of having so many great leaders in my career, there have only been a couple of toxic leaders with whom I have personally witnessed and interacted in my career. They were pitiful specimens as leaders, at best. By the time they left their organization, it was in shambles with a poor reputation from both a mission and culture standpoint. Due to the nature of their actions being so unpredictable, they are the most dangerous challenge in your personal leadership journey. You have to be aware of them and try to avoid organizations where they appear, since their leadership strategy and style are condoned.

Are You Bad? Despite best efforts by some to support these type of toxic leaders and make them successful, Kellerman (2004) puts forth the notion that Bad Leaders are in place only because they have followers who empower them. She calls them "Bad Followers". This is certainly a novel perspective and in her book she lays out scenarios where even leaders who are strong in some areas can be bad leaders in a very big way in selected blind spots. I look into that theory in a little more detail in a LinkedIn article I posted (2016 Dec 12). The last thing anyone should want to do is to empower a bad leader. So for these "king makers", do both yourself and the organization a favor – leave quickly. Do not be a "bad follower". If enough people leave, management a level above that toxic leader will have to take notice.

Everything you do in your career is a choice. If you choose to do nothing – by definition that is a choice. Instead, go to an organization where you can make positive contributions, make a difference, and most importantly – support your personal mission statement. It all starts there.

3. Not interested in paying market value or above for their employees. As mentioned in earlier discussion, some leaders actually believe that employees should want to stay in their organizations just because they are good people, and everyone should follow them to execute their mission since they are the leaders. As referenced in the employee surveys, salary and benefits has remained the #1 priority of employees for both leaving and for staying with an organization. This is

a reality that must be reckoned with by leaders. To do otherwise further jeopardizes the effectiveness of the organization.

Mr. or Ms. Slave Driver. I have seen two organizations where they believed that they were some type of "sole source" provider of jobs when nothing could be further from the truth. As a result their pay lagged behind other competing organizations, and they lost employees.

From observation, I believe they thought like in the time of the mid-1900's that people would not change organizations or – okay are you sitting down? Or that they would not move for another job? "Surely no one would actually move to an organization in another town or state!" I even heard one leader say that if people didn't want to work in the organization they "could get a job at Kmart". Sheesh! Some people live in a parallel universe.

That toxic thought must be flushed. If people produce, they must be paid. Show them appreciation – sure; engage them - absolutely. But really – show them the money! They are trying to look out for what is best for their family. If they do not produce – that's a different issue entirely.

Before we leave the topic, I want to encourage you to read *Good to Great*. In it, the author puts forth several novel concepts such as getting the right people on the bus which you manage (2001, Collins). However, a key takeaway from the book I would like to point out is that a strong leader will focus on their organization, and not themselves. By extension, if they are focusing on the organization, they are focusing on their people also. If you ever get to hear a leader speak, you will get a very good idea what type of leader they are if you look for these cues. Is the speech all about them, or is credit deflected to his or her people?

Chapter 16

TOXIC TRAP #2 - TOXIC EMPLOYEES

Most people who go to work every day are good people who want to put in their time, and want to have and display a degree of workmanship in which both they and their company will be proud. They want to give 100%, and be a part of a winning team. They also want to get along with the people who work next to them, and try to please their boss.

But in the years and environment where more and more employees have become free agents due to the structure of the pension systems, the free agent status of many has caused changes in company loyalty. People have to self-fund their own pensions. (More on that later.) Additionally, it has caused some negative changes in individual attitudes by a significant margin. Again, most workers are good citizens of their time, effort, and attitude. However, for this discussion, just like with toxic leaders, I will discuss toxic employees and break them down into three groupings.

1. Those who believe they are entitled. For some reason, there are more and more people today who believe that they should be given things such as added pay, promotions, better office and seating assignments and potentially more responsibility just because they have worked at the organization for a certain defined period of time. This is a transgenerational trend. In more isolated areas with smaller

populations it is not so prevalent. However, in larger population centers that have more organizations which compete for the same kind of labor, the workers do understand that if they want to walk out, they can and will land in another job.

You Owe Me. But this is more than a supply and demand issue, though it cannot be discounted. It is a major contributing factor. However, younger (and older employees) who enter the workforce believe they should be given pay advances and promotions every year. After five or six years some may have their pay maxed out unless they go into management.

This is contrasted with top scholastic performers coming out of the Ivy League Business Schools. You really cannot compare them due to the difference in expectations. I have had the opportunity to be in leadership class with Ivy School graduates, and those coming out in the top of their classes are given incredible responsibilities at an extremely young age. Whatever they get from a salary standpoint, it is my view that they earn and very much deserve. They are expected to produce and, more often than not, they can be counted on. They are compensated for the daily, constant pressure on them. If they do not produce, they are removed.

Back to the entitled group – this pervasive attitude described earlier causes these employees to perform at less than 100%, generally. Employees who have great attitudes and produce are the ones who usually get the prime responsibility jobs, and so those giving less are usually not picked. Therefore, the entitled bunch (not picked) begin to get defensive and start to complain. They whine to anyone who will listen. If there is a complaint management program, they complain. If there are employees sitting next to them, they complain. If there is a

Union, they complain. If there are unconstrained "open door policies" they complain.

This is an incredible drain on morale of the entire organization, and sucks the time and energy out of management as they have to deal with all of the complaints instead of production related challenges or issues. These whiners are people that management very much wishes would walk away and take another job. There are several human resource costing professionals who can prove out that the actual value of the contributions of this type of employee is negative. Let me restate. They do not add value to the mission of the organization, even if they provide some level of production of service or product. They subtract value. They are totally non-positive just because of the complaints aspect and the aforementioned drain.

2. Those who believe they owe no demonstrable effort or product to their company, customer, or team. This usually encompasses the first group as well. If someone believes they are entitled, their desire to contribute is less than optimal.

Intentionally Slacking. Therefore, not only is there a non-positive value associated to them because they complain, but it goes even further into the negative ledger because their actual contributions and performance nowhere near where they need to be. In many cases, their incomplete assignments and problems created with customer relationships require another level of management to intervene and reassign any number of personnel to address the performance deficiency of this type of employee. Depending on the deficiency severity it may cause multiple levels of management involvement.

As far as lackluster performance on work teams in the office, their lack of performance causes problems also with their co-workers. Therefore, everything they touch has problems and there is no place that this person can be logically assigned to be productive – or even isolated. If legal counsel will support, this type of person should be given an improvement requirement period. If that does not encourage the employee to work at an acceptable level, escalated personnel options should be pursued to eliminate them from the workforce.

3. Those who like to cause misery (misery loves company) and mistrust. Then there are employees who are their happiest when they are the saddest, or just plain miserable. These people are rarely happy at work, and the only time they have enjoyment is when they are stirring things up.

Miserable and Mean. While sometimes these employees do not have a sufficient workload, in many cases these employees can perform acceptably. They may not be star performers, but they will not have major deficiencies in their performance. They just like being unhappy and making other people like them. Often, they target management with behind the back conversation that is less than flattering, since it is sometimes easy for them to find a potentially sympathetic ear on the work floor. Other times, co-workers will find their ire. They are hard to predict. But you should be aware of them.

If there is any way possible, try to find others for friendship instead of these kinds of workers. It does not mean you should not record any known interests in your notes and try to work on a relationship (not necessarily close) should the opportunity occur. But do not get sucked in by a person with this behavior. Sometimes they can become contagious. If you fall prey to their games, they can become toxic to you and your career.

Chapter 17

TOXIC TRAP #3 - TOXIC LABOR-MANAGEMENT RELATIONSHIPS

Labor Unions have had a place in American History as they began to protect workers when industrial manufacturers and companies mismanaged their human capital in the earlier part of the 20th century. They treated them poorly, overworked them, and often put them in very unsafe conditions. Due to Unions, and their efforts to safeguard employee rights and safety, many positive changes have taken place with the American workers. There are many workplace rules and regulations in place that help protect workers and keep them safe without abusive treatment.

Having a good relationship with Unions, where Unions are applicable, will be an advantageous accomplishment. If there is a bargaining unit which has voted to have a Union, what better way to gain buy-in on new and emerging workforce policy or changes in production standards from employees than getting the Union on board to help sell the concept. No matter what change there is, if you have another recognizable advocate that helps with the trust issue, it certainly would be best to go that route.

Trust and Communication. I have had the opportunity to be a part of a Labor-Management Partnership Council where there was extensive trust. Even though, not required, many opportunities for information and participation were afforded to the Labor officers due to the trust they had earned with Management. Similarly, the Union worked to convey positive perspectives on many changes being put to the workforce.

The negotiation of the Labor-Management Agreement during this time period was somewhat tense. As a matter of fact, the tentative agreement was broken by the Union before it was signed. A mediator was called in to assist final resolution. But that experience and the ability to establish common ground was huge. Without common ground, it would not have been possible to establish a good relationship. It was out of that establishment of common ground that the Partnership was formed.

My personal experiences have given me the opportunity to be part of a management-labor partnership on behalf of management with three different Unions. Fortunately, two of them were very positive and produced many positive management and workforce outcomes.

Be Very Aware of Agendas. I have also had the experience of dealing with a Labor-Union which did not have common ground with the organization. They had other ideas and agendas. Unfortunately, the ability to communicate the importance of mission was either not understood or was not deemed relevant by that particular Union. Management desired to treat employees well, but agenda issues blocked an effective relationship. For the most part, the lower level officers in the Union were very warm, friendly, and compassionate and smaller win/wins for both management and employees were found there through communication. That was despite barriers put in place by the Labor leadership.

It just needs to be noted that this is an issue which could be an obstacle to your career success unless you are aware of it. Again, communication is a key here. If you do not have to be part of this issue or get involved where there is toxicity, take care of yourself, your mission statement execution, and your career. Most people want to get along and take the high road. Stay on that high road, and watch out for detours that could hurt you and your career.

PART 6

KEEPING ON THE HIGH ROAD TO SUCCESS

Chapter 18

PREDICTION OF ORGANIZATIONAL CULTURE

How can you tell if an organization has an effective culture or a toxic culture? There are many thoughts about this. Earlier we saw that a leader may or may not even know that there is a problem, but if there is a problem it is the leader who has to lead the change to make it positive. That too is a choice – of the leader.

If you are already part of the organization, you know the answer to what the culture is like. However, if you are not, it is a mystery. You can talk with a person or two who works there. But then you are relying on a survey of one or two people out of however many people who work for the organization. This is not a statistically sound sample from which to base a conclusion.

I would like to put forth the theory that a lot can be gleaned by the degree an organization participates in community service. One of the areas that is measured by the Malcolm Baldrige Criteria is the degree to which an organization has community service participation. From a theory standpoint, there is much said about a company being a responsible citizen. It is always different words but it says mostly the same thing. (Scholarships, picking up litter, Advocacy for children, helping soup kitchens, etc.) These are all very worthy things.

But I have never seen an analysis of what that really means for the culture or even more – I have never seen it suggested that this may actually show a correlation on how an organization's employees are treated.

I think this is an analytical breakthrough and linkage. Would it not be reasonable to assume that if a company invests its time and resources into helping the community by hosting an annual golf tournament or hosting a fundraising walk that they would also be interested in treating their employees well?

If you read on a company's website several volunteering efforts for the community, I would take notice. If they offer only a $100 scholarship once a year and that is the extent of it, I would also notice that, but not be particularly moved positively.

From past volunteer experiences, hosting a walk takes a lot of coordination. Hosting a golf tournament takes even more coordination and commitment. Both of them are huge investments of time. What if an organization does both? Are there pictures of the President of the company there? Are there events where the CEO is captured in picture making an address to the crowd at the event?

The degree to which the organization's leader is invested into the event, or events, is extremely telling. It would be totally counterintuitive to not take this in consideration. At some point, other theorists and Malcom Baldrige would do well to pick up this linkage. Virtually all community service affects others. If there is an investment by the organization's leader into people through community service, it is a reflection of that person's core values. Those core values will not change for the organization's employees or its customers.

Having organizational employees participate in events like this is very good. This gives you an idea that employees commit to charitable events sponsored by the organization. But having the senior leaders involved is the real key. By having their involvement, it becomes apparent that they are invested and like to have their company resources and employees invested as well.

I know there is always a positive public perception about community service. That is true, and it is a good thing, as it also sets an example. However, if a leader is not really invested into helping others in a big way, they are not going to subscribe to a great effort that maximizes human effort as a contribution. You will be able to ascertain this information from their website.

Even if others do not know about this correlation, use this to your advantage as you find the right fit for your personal mission statement.

Chapter 19

APPLICATION OF 3.6 LEADERSHIP

Imagine a picture of a house which has four columns on the front porch bracing the roof. The columns are well established by the foundation of the porch. Without the foundation, the columns and roof which it supports would fall.

The 3.6 Leadership concepts of Action, Attitude, Awareness, and Attraction represent the columns of new ideas and are based on the foundation of Communication (the porch). The roof covers everything you represent in life – both your personal and professional life. You can work on each of the four concepts individually from a sub-goal standpoint. However, without the support of Communication you cannot successfully accomplish any of them.

What happens if the owner decided to take down the columns to present a different look. What would happen to the roof? What if two columns were taken down? What about one column? There may be a way to brace the roof without one of the columns. But it would be extremely costly and complex to do it. So why would you want to do it? Use all of the columns to maximize the strength and stability of the roof – and of your success.

Communication, just like the porch, is the key; it is the foundation. It gives you the foundation to strive for success in each of the first four points, and you must have it to find success in your current or prospective job(s).

Most concepts in training forums are presented in ways which are easily remembered. For instance, Maslow's Hierarchy of Needs is represented with a pyramid. Even if one cannot remember the names of all the Needs in the Hierarchy, they remember the shape, and a person needing to climb the hierarchy of needs in order to self-actualize. It is all in attaching an image to easily represent the concept or theory.

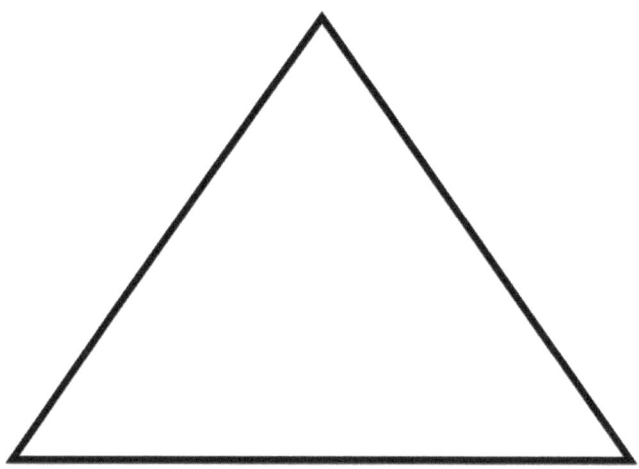

Pyramid representation

Additionally, I mentioned earlier in the book about Dr. Portera always using a rule of three (and sometimes four) when he was making oral presentation points. He wanted to articulate what could be simple, but profound, takeaways. If he named three, there is a good chance the audience would remember or be able to write it down, or capture it in their mobile device. If he named nine or ten points – no one would remember anything except how long his list was. His presentations usually were two types. One was for information purposes, and the other was some type of call for action (e.g. call for donations). In both cases, they were very focused.

That reminds me of a leadership conference I attended many years ago, and the conference speaker droned on for what seemed like hours. But I'm sure it was only 40 or 45 minutes – or was it? When he hit point #6 twice (actually two different points but he called out #6 (a second time) instead of #7), I could have just put my head down or clicked my heels three times wishing I were anywhere but listening to this person read his top 12 reasons (or was it 10) to do whatever topic he was - yammering – I mean- talking about. …And yes, he was reading his presentation with no charts, at least, to look at….

It is therefore, always a good lesson to give your audience a chance to remember the takeaway. If it is an oral presentation, be careful or you will lose your audience in thought. If it is a written piece, you have a little more latitude – but not much. However, you still want to leave the audience with some type of reference point to allow for ease of learning and recall, and any associated action, if that is applicable. If you cannot do that, you fail.

Therefore, the memory cue associated with 3.6 is simply this. Four of the items start with an "A" and one, Communication, starts with a "C". If this were a college semester course load of five subjects and three hours each, it would calculate to a 3.6. That's the hook. You can do the math to check – not the intent. However, anything to spark the memory IS the intent.

3.6 Leadership -

> **Action**
> **Attitude**
> **Awareness**

<u>A</u>ttraction of New Ideas
<u>C</u>ommunication

So 4 A's and 1 C. If you practice 3.6 Leadership in each organization you support, you are sure to find your path to success. But the choice is still yours. You have to choose. You must absolutely choose. Remember, doing nothing is a choice. Too often we choose to absolutely do nothing. That is a shame because it is a responsibility you cannot give away. It is yours to manage.

Success is not guaranteed, and it will neither be given to you just because you work hard and perhaps accomplish good things and outcomes currently, nor will jobs fall in your lap because you have done great work your whole career in two or three jobs. You have to take responsibility for your future, your mission, and your passion.

Since you took the time to read this book, I believe you have every intent to improve yourself and make adjustments as necessary to maximize your personal contributions at both work and at home. Keep learning and pushing, and never give up. No one can stop you. Only you can. Only you can drive your success. Only you can choose your path.

Chapter 20 was written with the express intent to continue with the encouragement of you as you choose to make changes in your life, and in your mission, to enable your career success. It will also provide added detail about the context from which I write.

The Afterword will show you how 3.6 Leadership has been applied in one of my new businesses of selling BBQ sauces made from my late wife's recipes. I also have a consulting business and it would be easier to show how 3.6 Leadership is applied there. But I would rather take up the challenge of showing you how 3.6 Leadership can be applied in the operation of a start-up business that is totally self-reliant.

FINAL CALLING

The inspiration for this book is my family, but has been based on my professional experiences, research and learning. I hope the information presented in the text has convinced you that you must start your journey to career success by writing your personal mission statement. I have decided to include added personal information to assist your deliberation in arriving at that conclusion, if you have not done so already. This is your final call.

This is too important for your career and life to not double down and get to this very important effort. After reading this, you will understand how important I believe it is to include it in every decision you make as a professional, and in your personal life. This is not information that I share lightly.

After an extremely long and courageous battle with an illness, my late wife, Candy, passed away on February 9, 2016. She was in the ICU at the University of Alabama at Birmingham (UAB) for seven consecutive months until all fight she had was completely exhausted. We were married 30 years and she was always my soulmate, and my #1 supporter. She was always the encourager to both our son, Wyatt, and me. She and I lived life together to its fullest, as wife and husband, as mom and dad - as one - and shared so many happy times, fun times, and went together thru so many tough times. But we never gave up hope for tomorrow.

As part of this fight, we moved closer to Birmingham in the summer of 2015 to cut a significant number of miles off of the round trips to UAB and back. The impact to Wyatt was he had to transfer high schools his senior year. While this was tough on Wyatt, he knew how serious the stakes were, and he willingly agreed to the move. Both of his schools (the one he left and the one he attended as a senior) had families and staff that were incredibly supportive of both Wyatt and Candy and me. I could talk about how the Madison Academy (MA) family supported Wyatt through Wyatt's 11th grade year and beyond, and many hours about how the Decatur Heritage Christian Academy family supported Wyatt and me during his very tough senior year.

It seemed apropos that both MA and Decatur Heritage baseball teams and families were at the State Championship series in Montgomery to win the championship in their respective classifications in May of 2016. What happened was the MA family began to rally around Wyatt (who played for the MA baseball team while attending there) and Decatur Heritage (he played for them his senior year) and cheered for them. For me personally, it was extremely overwhelming considering all that had taken place with our family. That experience, articulated with so much love, will never be forgotten.

The purpose of this, though, is not to detail all of the tough times. Those are times that no one can either know or understand. Further, on one added note, I have come to the realization that no one can know what anyone else is experiencing in a personal loss because of the fact that no one else has had that relationship. Absolutely no one. You can offer people words of encouragement – and always offer encouragement. That is always a positive thing to do! But please don't ever say to someone who has had any type of loss or tragedy, "I know what you are going through." No one else has had that relationship!

Candy and I have both been followers of Jesus and I know that Candy is in Heaven now cooking up a great meal on her double oven for Wyatt and me even as I write this, made even more special with the love that I know she has for us also. She was the best cook on this earth, so I am sure she is testing her cooking prowess there as well!

What I will do now is list some of the happiest times Candy had during our marriage. (There is a purpose, so stick with me.)

1. Wyatt, our son, is #1 by far the greatest source of happiness to both Candy and me. He was always a joy to her, and certainly is a joy to me. She was Wyatt's team mom in baseball for several years and nothing gave her more joy than watching Wyatt on the baseball field pitching, hitting, or competing because she knew how much he loved playing. It did not matter if he won or lost. She always did everything she could to make sure he had everything he needed growing up – even when she did not feel well.

2. Getting married. I'm glad it made the list! We had a tremendous marriage. Again, it was a love and relationship that no one can comprehend because – it was our relationship. It was a relationship we worked at, and we kept as our priority. Yep – we had tough times. But we had great times!

    (Similarly, no one can know the depths of the relationships you have.)

3. Wyatt choosing his college. When Wyatt went through his very methodical process in choosing his college, it made Candy so very happy. Our timetable was that Wyatt would choose his school by the end of November in 2015. After that, we would ensure all

efforts and focus were doubled to get Candy out of the hospital and home – or to another hospital where she could recover and then come home. When Wyatt told us together those infamous words, "I'm going to Brevard". It made Candy so happy. The reason for the happiness was not the choice of school per se, though the mountains of North Carolina was our favorite place. But it was the process. I had taken short day trips with Wyatt to all of the schools he visited except for one of them. My report back to Candy was so positive on every one of the schools. I told her, "When I was 17, I would have signed at the first school we visited". Each time he visited a college, I told Candy I thought that is where Wyatt was going to go. This was highly unusual for Candy to see me so indecisive. She thought it was funny. Again, seeing Wyatt go thru that process made Candy so happy. She knew at that point, Wyatt would be alright. He made such a big decision for 17 years old. She knew he had the ability to make adult decisions for the rest of his life, and it was something she did not have to worry about any more.

4. Her getting to see Wyatt play at Delta State. In the summer of 2014 (and 2015), Wyatt played showcase ball for Team Mississippi. One showcase was at Delta State University, where Candy graduated. This was the first time she had been to the tiny town of Cleveland, Mississippi and to her campus in 30 years. To be able to see Wyatt play here, was a dream for her. He was recovering from an arm injury during the summer of 2014 and could only be a designated hitter to protect his arm. However, he came up big and led his team to rally to beat the #1 team in the country in one of the games at the woodbat showcase. Her joy was exceedingly great that weekend. Being back on campus – an improved and larger campus, and an improved town with more places to eat – with her boy on the DSU Diamond – it couldn't get much better for her.

Wyatt on first base at Delta State after getting a hit against the #1 team in the country in 2014. Candy watching it all.

5. 10-year anniversary surprise trip. When we were planning (I should say I was planning) the trip, I told Candy the destination was going to be a surprise. A week before departure time, I told Candy she needed to pack her bathing suit, and her sweats and sweaters. She said, "what do you mean?" I replied that "we were either going to a place where you will need your bathing suit, or your sweats and sweaters." I believe she was stunned to the level of the surprise. So away we flew out of the Mobile, Alabama airport. She asked if we were going to North Carolina "again". We loved to go to the mountains – it was our favorite place - but she said, "I don't want to go to North Carolina for my 10- year anniversary!" I told her I couldn't say. Well, she got worked up a bit over that reply. We transferred planes in Atlanta and only when we landed in Buffalo she said, "We are going to Niagara Falls, aren't we?" I told her I still couldn't say. We got in our rental car and came to the Niagara

Falls exit and I just kept driving past it. She said, "Where are we going?" I told her I couldn't say. After about 15 minutes and well into Canada, I took an exit and said, "Yes. We are going to Niagara Falls."

We had the best time. It was absolutely awesome with so much beauty. We went on the Maid of the Mist, went behind the Falls, and ate at the restaurant which was on a revolving floor on the top floor of a building. There are too many things to talk about for this purpose, but it was a great trip and an even greater surprise and memory.

6. San Diego trip. This was a trip where I went to a Leadership class in 2009, and I was able to take both Candy and Wyatt. I had been to San Diego a couple of times before so I had a feel for the area. There were many things which Candy and Wyatt did during the day while I was in training, such as going to the Aquarium and the Zoo. (Apparently, Candy even got in "trouble" for petting restricted marine life at the Aquarium (LOL).) They also made it to Lego Land. But I took advantage of the weekends before and after the class to ensure we went to SeaWorld, the Wildlife Refuge, and to a Padres game where Wyatt got a baseball autographed by some of the Padres. Awesome trip. We all loved everything about it. If the cost of housing were not so high there….

7. Every birthday party, Halloween party, baseball party, and every other imaginable reason to have a get together at the house, wherever we lived – especially for Wyatt. She loved Wyatt and doing for Wyatt, and she loved kids. She always made all the parties so fun. For one Halloween party when Wyatt was eight years old, he wanted to be Darth Maul. If you don't know who Darth Maul is I guess you haven't been to any movies this Century…. When she finished with the incredible makeup job, it was a true work of art (and love). When

Wyatt looked in the mirror it actually scared him. The evidence of the Darth Maul project follows.

Candy and Darth Maul aka Wyatt – Halloween 2006

8. 1st night in the house we built, complete with surprise furniture. We built a house on the Coast in 1998 and moved in during January of 1999. We loved our 11 years on the Coast. There were so many good friends and stories. When we were moving into the house, Candy didn't know I had bought this bedroom suite she had been looking at from a furniture company in Biloxi. It was one she really liked, but she thought it wasn't in our budget due to building the house. She was absolutely thrilled to get that furniture, and move into the house that we built. Wyatt was eight months old when we moved in. Wyatt and I had a chance in March of 2016 to revisit the Coast and the house where he grew up, along with old friends. Lots of happy times, friends, and memories.

9. Wyatt winning the Mother's Day tournament for Candy in 2010. Wyatt was playing travel baseball with a nice group of kids and

families from Morgan County, Alabama at the time. This was their first year together and they had a lot of fun, but lost about as much as they won. As it turned out at the "Mother's Day Off" tournament, the team was playing well, and they got to the semifinals. The umpire had a small strike zone and our starting pitcher had run out of gas. We had a two or three run lead and our pitcher started walking kids. There were two outs in the last inning with a 2-1 count on the batter and the coach put Wyatt in mid-at bat. Wyatt had already pitched so he was on a short pitch count. He threw two pitches, both strikes to that batter to strike the kid out. On to the Championship game.

As most tournaments do, they run late and this was no exception. The championship game was starting just after 10:00PM. At midnight, it would be Mother's Day. There were a lot of runs scored on both sides. There was one kid on the other team who was just pounding the ball when he batted. He hit the fence in left field and he hit the fence in right field in consecutive at bats, and he got on base every time he batted. Our pitching was all used up, but Wyatt who had just a few pitches left in his count should he be needed. We were winning by two runs in the next to last inning and there were two outs, and the pitcher from our team loaded the bases with walks. He wasn't even close to the plate. Guess who was up to bat next for the other team? Yep – "the kid". The coach brought Wyatt in to face "the kid", and he ran the count full at 3-2. You couldn't walk him, it would force in a run. The tension was pretty high at that point! He then struck out "the kid". Wow! The team and fans (parents) were so fired up. The last inning there was one kid who got a hit off Wyatt, and Wyatt then picked him off of 1st. All during the last inning and a half, Candy was pacing back and forth, back and forth. When Wyatt registered the last out, the clock struck midnight. After the dog pile - Happy Mother's Day, Mom - from Wyatt!

Wyatt and team after winning Mother's Day
Off Tournament in 2010. Wyatt is #5.

10. Surprise 40th birthday party. Candy had never had a birthday party growing up as a kid, and usually our celebrations at home were quite private. But on this one, I was determined it was going to be the mother of all parties. I planned it with the help of some very close friends from central Mississippi, and even got her mother to play along with the ruse. It was incredible. It was attended by family and friends from near and far, and she was very surprised. She could not believe that this party had been done for her. She was thrilled! Wyatt was a little more than two years old at the time, and of course he never met a group of people where he couldn't find someone

to play with. He wound up playing with his cousins the whole time. What a great time for all!

11. Acapulco trip. This was pre-Wyatt and was while I was working in New Orleans. During my commutes it actually gave me an opportunity to pick up Spanish and there were enough Latin people at work that I got to practice it. Tip #1 – never fly thru the Mexico City airport if you absolutely do not have to. If I were not able to speak Spanish I do not know how we would have found the correct terminal when we changed planes. There were so many people, and there were goats. – No, not the "greatest of all time"…. Goats! Stinkin' Goats! Well we finally got to our connection, arrived in Acapulco and took a taxi to our Casita at Las Brisas. What a view of the Pacific! It was so beautiful. We bought several things from the market place including the silver cross I wear occasionally. The best food we had? Hard Rock Café. Authentic Mexican food may not have been our favorite thing! But the parasailing she did was great – other than that big rock they almost flew her into! :>O What an adventure it was. We also got to see cliff divers from the restaurant where Elvis was in a movie. So much fun – and did I say we had our own private pool?

12. Snow days Christmas 2010. On Christmas Eve we had to race back home to Madison, Alabama from my Mother's as the Snow Storm of 2010 started moving in earlier than predicted. It was a solid 5 ½ hours on the best of days. That day it took 6 ½ hours. Just before we hit the Tennessee River Bridge it hit 32 degrees. While we were driving carefully, some nutcase flew past us on the bridge and started to fishtail. Fortunately, they didn't wreck and we stayed far away from them as they slid past us.

The six inches of snow were incredible. Candy loved the snow more than any other type of weather event. We took a lot of pictures – and then the fun started. Snowball fights. Neighborhood snowball fights. Finally got to use the boogey board (never used it at the beach). But it made a great sled going down hills and driveways.…. Candy made snow ice cream and warm stew. What great memories and Wyatt was also in the center of them.

13. Jacksonville trip for New Years 2011. We went to Jacksonville, Florida for the Gator Bowl just 5 days after our white Christmas. Just like every other football game we attended, the games are always fun, but all of the activities surrounding the game are really where you have the quantity of fun that you remember. The entire trip was fantastic. The temperature was in the 70s just five days after we were experiencing 25 degrees back home. Our room was right on the Atlantic Ocean. The Gulf is nice; but the Ocean (either) is literally so majestic and awesome! We fished, shopped, saw things, ate great food, even chased the MSU football bus down the interstate as they were literally "flying" to go to their private practice facility at one of the colleges in Jacksonville. Why did we follow? Well – why not? We just had fun. MSU wound up thrashing Michigan and that made for more fun. After the game, Wyatt got autographs and Candy even took a picture with one of the football players. LOL. We hated to go back home to 40-degrees. But we had a blast while we were there.

14. Wyatt's all-star team winning district and going to state when he was 10. This was Wyatt's last year playing league ball and it looked like the odds were stacked against us – or so that was the word on the street. The other team had a couple of very good pitchers and apparently, the families were already booking reservations for state. That rubbed the moms on our team the wrong way just a bit. Baseball moms do get excited!

But what did we do? We practiced hard, learned to bunt, and got ready for a three-game series (best two out of three). Of course, Candy had all the moms wearing the same type of clothing and had signs and such. Anything to support the team. In the first inning the lead-off kid on our team got a triple and Wyatt came up to bat. I gave him the bunt sign (I was the coach), and he laid down the most perfect bunt ever, despite the fact he had never laid down a bunt in any game before that moment. Everyone at the park (including the other team, our team families, and Candy) except Wyatt and I, and our other coaches were stunned. He easily got to first with a hit and no throw and the run scored. We took a lot of pitches, laid down several bunts and wound up winning pretty big in game one. Since they burned their top two pitchers in game one, we went on to win game two and were heading to state. Candy was so thrilled. She then coordinated our reservations – after we won. It just seems like yesterday.…

15. Camping adventures. We had a couple of campers. The first was a pop-up and we bought it when Wyatt was two. How hard can it be to use a pop up, right? Well as it turns out I tested that theory. We were camping in Destin and had a long day at the beach, and doing things outside in the sun and heat. Wyatt was playing with either his construction equipment or his Thomas trains on the floor of the pop-up and I decided I would lay down for a minute while he tired himself out. (I was already tired.) Candy was already on the bed reading and so when I sat down on the other side of her at the far end, the camper tilted to that end. Yes – one end was 45 degrees in the air! In a flash, I hopped off the bed back on the floor and the end in the sky went back to the ground. LOL – tho I was too stunned to laugh immediately. I went outside and the people in the driving RV next to us (one that cost well into the six figures) were outside laughing so hard I thought I was going to

have to call the paramedics for them. Apparently, there is a brace under each end of the pop-ups that must be deployed – so one end will not go down with the other in the air. Obviously, in my haste to pick up the camper I blew off the whole instructions part of it as it would be easy to figure out….

Then we sold the pop-up and bought a 28-foot travel trailer. If this one popped in the air, we would definitely be in some serious trouble! We camped primarily in the Smoky Mountains in several places, loving every one of them. We also camped several times at Lake Lowndes just outside Columbus, Mississippi for football game weekends at Mississippi State. This is a state park that is off the beaten path and it was a lot of fun. We would take our bicycles, fishing rod and reel, football, baseball and gloves, and just had a blast. Candy would always fix us the best food and the air conditioning made for some good sleeping while camping. Staying in clean quarters, and not behind people in hotels was really a major plus for Candy. So many great memories.

Candy called me at work one day and out of the blue said, "Can I sell the camper?" I said, "Sure" – knowing it would take a long time (probably weeks) to sell and it would give me time to talk her out of it. I knew the last couple of trips had been a hassle since we had to keep the camper in storage due to homeowners' covenants. On the Coast, we could just pull it behind the house on our land. I got home and Candy announced, "our camper is sold; let's go meet the people at our storage facility." I was speechless as I drove there and took the check from the people and gave them the keys. Later – much later - all I could was laugh….

Honorable mention – our one million trips to Orlando! You all know about it as you have all gone. We enjoyed central Florida from Tampa to Cocoa Beach. Lots of happy times!

Having read this, how can you not have your own personal mission statement defined, written, and in use? You work to live; you do not live to work. Think about what is really important to you, and to those you love and care for. Do not miss out on what is important. This is your life and you only have one shot.

When I have conducted Leadership sessions in the past I have always had a slide of Leadership perspectives. On that slide I lay out what is important to me, as a manager. In the very center of it I have a "Gold Box". In the box, I have two things written – "Family" and "Customers". I go on to explain to those receiving the presentation that if you do not have your relationships right with your family, you have no chance of doing a good job, or effective job, of communicating and meeting your customers' needs. I know that is a revolutionary thought, and I guarantee it is not in MGT 201, 301, 401, or 601. But I have found that to be true – and I was just not giving it lip service.

So I say the same thing to you – if you do not have your relationships right - in the Gold Box, true success is not going to happen for you, and you will have regrets later in life. Your choice. I call this the Gold Box Principle, and part of the Value Driven Purpose which is illustrated on the following page. All of the elements of this have been discussed in these pages.

Work is all about choices, just like life. How do you know you are in the right job? I think you know now after you have read this book and have at least drafted your personal mission statement. By following principles in this book, you should now have a written plan to get you to your right job - if you are not already there. Once you are in your right job, you have a strategy and plan to be successful at work with the principles of 3.6 Leadership and Leadership Marketing.

But it all starts with your focus on what takes place outside of the 8 to 5 – in the Gold Box. I sincerely wish you the best as you apply these principles for your life and success.

Wyatt and me after his team won the state baseball championship – his 3d consecutive championship - with 2 schools. This was May of 2016.

Candy and me at her brother and sister-in-law's wedding in 1997.

APPLICATION OF 3.6 LEADERSHIP IN CANDY'S FOODS

During the fall of 2016 I set out to organize Candy's cook books. Some the binding had been broken and there were loose pages – some intentional for repetitive use, but most unintentional. While going through the recipes, I found her recipes for BBQ sauces. The Sweet sauce was the absolute best I have ever tasted, and I decided that I was going to produce them for market distribution.

I decided that I was also going to consult, so I set up an LLC and had a DBA incorporated under the LLC for Candy's Foods. That way I could have one taxable organization and be able to track expenses separately. Getting the legal part of this accomplished was a challenge and I used Legal Zoom to assist in the navigation. The LLC went smoothly, but the DBA not so much.

The website was a headache. In the process I used Go Daddy, Vista Print, and Shopify, with the latter being the only platform which gave me what I needed to track municipality and state taxes. Taxes had to be tracked to ensure tax receipts were reimbursed to the right jurisdictions. The whole website construction cannot be understated. It was very difficult, and I did it by myself on all three occurrences.

Licensing was very confusing. There are sales tax licenses for state, county, and city, and there is also vendor registration federally to obtain an EIN number. Oh – and you have to submit sales tax returns monthly whether anything is owed or not. Federally and for state, you have to file quarterly if you owe income tax.

Choosing a logo took weeks and weeks as I wanted to ensure the right logo, trademark, and name, and then to seek protection. I coordinated with good friends and Wyatt's input was also very valuable to the process. After consideration and consultation with an intellectual property attorney, I submitted my design to the Office of Patents and Trademark (OPT). They came back with comments. In response, I got dozens of law firms spamming me saying they were the only ones who could help me. I responded to all three of the concerns myself – and successfully. In return, the OPT came up with a new concern. So I got spammed again. I will respond myself on this one too.

I also went thru a hard drive crash during this time. That required rework and impacted my cost tracking significantly, but I pushed through.

As part of my outreach and marketing I have targeted four types of stores: a) gourmet shops, b) gift shops, c) florists with gift shops, and d) pharmacies with gift shops. Moreover, I have online sales, and I am working a booth at select festival type events.

I am trying to deliver most of the products to customers. I know this is costing a little more, but I think it is important to create good customer relationships up front. I want the sauce to taste good, and everything about the business to be a positive.

I have also encountered a major supplier snag as my provider of commercial kitchen equipment unexpectedly went out of business. This is a very significant hurdle as it has shot a hole in my business model.

So how does 3.6 Leadership apply?

1. Action – There have been so many overwhelming and complex moving parts to this venture. While making customer relationships has been challenging, it has been one of the more gratifying things. However, website construction, licensing, getting a trademark, filing taxes, establishing a supplier to assist with bottling, each have been disruptive enough to make one think twice about establishing a business. None of these have been user friendly.

However, being proactive, and creating opportunities and relationships have been key. I have even used lessons learned from other friends have either been in business, or are still operating businesses. Take action and learn – but you have to keep consistent action and pressure on issues until they are complete. There are no exceptions to this. That is what I have tried to do.

2. Attitude - How key has attitude been with establishing relationships with all of the key players. I probably did not lose my cool except with Vista Print – and they are the nicest people. However, they are not fast in any way, and what they say they can give you is not always what they give you. But you should always keep a good attitude and show appreciation. Without question that has been key to getting a lot of helpful advice that I have been able to apply.

Determining shipping partners was even a very difficult decision which took weeks. I chose UPS over the U.S. Postal Service due to their extended hours and flexibility in arrangements for shipping. Also, their customer service line, and a local UPS Store have made shipping a positive part of the business platform. Keeping a good attitude has made all the difference in the world.

3. Awareness – Understanding clearly what my personal mission is, and what my mission was with this business was something in which I am aware, and further I have a strong passion (vision) for this business. Candy loved life and cooking and I am sharing a part of that with others.

But if I did not have such a passion, I would probably not have made it through the first barrier or challenge. The rules and requirements of everything involved in operating a business is incredible. A small business person has to be so well versed in so many different skillsets.

4. Attraction of New Ideas – Without New Ideas in this business, I guess I would have nothing but the recipes. Everything is new to me, and just like on the websites, I have had to make adjustments.

Another area is that I was given the idea to attach one of Candy's recipes to each bottle of sauce. I had to figure out how to deliver that in a sustainable and repeatable method. So I went to Michael's to see about ideas. I got a decent idea, but it was not repeatable. I had completed about 10 tags in 3 hours. Nope. That wouldn't work. So I took it in a different direction that worked.

I had the same thing that happened with packing bottles. I had to try different approaches to ensure safety of product. Adjustments were made. But I ran into a wall when I started packing 12 to a box with the recipe tags. I knew how to pack it when I had 12 to a box without the tags. But they are so small I couldn't conceive that it would make a difference in packing.

So away I go, packing 12 in the box just like I did before the recipe tags were added. It didn't fit. So I unpacked, and packed it again the same way. Wow – it still didn't fit! So I unpacked it, and packed it again – for the 3d time - the same way. "There must be something I am doing wrong…." About this time Wyatt saw me perplexed over this unsolvable mystery and he said, "I have an idea. Why don't you do it like this?" He then visually showed me what his thoughts were. I said OK and away I went to packing. They fit! What if I had said, "No. This is how I've always done it and I must be doing something wrong." I guess I would still be packing that box….

There is no question you have to be flexible, and in almost every part of the business I am making adjustments. I am doing this even with how I present my products at the festival events. I will not go into that detail, but I have learned a trick or two by watching others at events.

I also had fun with the 5th sauce – a new add – "Don't Fear the Reaper Q-Kick Sauce". I took one of Candy's base recipes and mixed in the Carolina Reaper Pepper which is the hottest pepper in the world at this writing. The last three shows I did, I set up a "Don't Fear the Reaper Experience". All 57 people that took the challenge loved it. Booths around me stopped to watch every time it occurred. Lots of fun!

5. Communication – To accomplish anything with the business I have had to leverage every type of communication for which I have had access. Customer service lines, managers in tax offices, friends, new friends in stores, others in the sauce business (even developed a mentor relationship), and others who have had tremendous ideas….

Any success with the business to date has been a result of communication. Relationships with potential stores usually take a while. Sometimes it can take weeks. In one case it has taken several months. It is also something you cannot rush. Being flexible with your communications and approach is important for these relationships. At this point, the sauce is in 26 stores in 6 states.

So at the end of the day – I am using 3.6 Leadership in my business for all operational aspects. Without it, I would not be able to succeed. With it, I have structure, focus and am very excited about the future.

Bibliography

Cascio, W., Young, C. & and Morris, J., (1997). *Financial Consequences of Employment Change Decisions in Major U.S. Corporations.* Academy of Management Journal 40(5), 1175-1189.

Collins, J., (2001). *Good to Great.* HarperCollins.

Covey, S., (2013). *The 7 Habits of Highly Effective People, Anniversary Edition,* New York: Simon and Schuster.

Eades, J., (2017, January 10). *The Disastrous Problem Revenue Doesn't Solve.* LinkedIn.

Farrior, C. (2003, July). *The Management of Downsizing Risk.* Contract Management. 26-31.

Farrior, C., (2011, May 11). *How Can Civilian Retention in the Army Contracting Command Contracting Professional Community be Affected? (Research Paper supporting presentation to Naval Postgraduate School Research Symposium.)*

Farrior, C. (2016, July 13). *Who Will Take Your Box?* LinkedIn.

Farrior, C. (2016, December 12). *Are You Considered Bad?* LinkedIn.

Heathfield, S., *Top Ten Ways to Retain Your Great Employees. Why Retention? Four Tips for Employee Retention.* Retrieved August 6, 2010 from www.humanresources.about.com.

Houston, B., (2015) *Live Love Lead,* New York: FaithWords, p. 36.

Kellerman, B., (2004) *Bad Leadership,* Boston, Massachusetts: Harvard Business School Publishing.

Little, L., (2013) *Make A Difference,* Indiana: iUniverse.

Merhar, C., (2016, Feb. 4). *Employee Retention – The Real Cost of Losing an Employee.* Small Business Employee Benefits and HR Blog. Retrieved January 8, 2017 from www.zanebenefits.com.

Pink, D., (2009) *Drive. The Surprising Truth about What Motivates Us.* New York, NY: Riverhead Books.

Towers Watson, (2010). *Creating a Sustainable Rewards and Talent Management Model: Results of the 2010 Global Talent Management and Rewards Study.* Retrieved at towerswatson.com.

Willis Towers Watson, (2016). *Under pressure to remain relevant, employers look to modernize the employee value proposition Global findings report for the Results of the 2016 Global Talent Management and Rewards and Global Workforce Studies.* Retrieved at willistowerswatson.com.

Acknowledgements

As you might expect, acknowledgements start at home and in many ways, I have already addressed this. But I give my wife credit for my success. Even, though, she has passed on from this life, I know we will see each other again by the grace of our Lord and Savior, Jesus. Her strength and love, and her memory give me courage to try to make an impact on others.

My son, Wyatt, is my inspiration. I will, and always will, do everything I can to support him, love him, cheer for him, be his advocate, and just make sure he has every opportunity to be successful in life. I will still support him, no matter what. But he has to choose his path. He will have to make choices that ultimately affect his destiny. He is in his sophomore year in college as I complete this, and he made his choice as to where to go to college for his freshman year, (and made another choice for his sophomore year.) It was a tough process, but he made the choice with the skill of an adult. It was a process that made his mom and me very happy and proud of him. He has now chosen he will go to school his junior and senior years at Mississippi State University. #HAILSTATE

There have been so many friends, family members, and close friends made both away from work and at work, both leaders and those working for me. They are far too many to name and list the reasons, the moments of reflection, the good times, and the tough times…. They are from every place we lived and worked, and from where we went to church. They are also from every walk of life, demographic, and background. Some are also connected by association of Wyatt's teams. Lots of good friends from the ball fields and basketball courts.

I have also had the distinct honor of working with many men and women in both the Army and Navy. They have all just been incredible, and I have learned much from working with them, leading them, and supporting them. They are the top character group anywhere around. Their passion for what they do, what they sacrifice, and what they risk is unparalleled. They should be the most respected group, bar none.

I have learned across the years, everything is not always black and white. You always take just a little something to grow on from every relationship, from every job, from every issue, and from every stage of life. You learn from all of that. It is the relationships I cherish, and I do my part to try to stay in contact with friends as best as I can. Keep learning, keep believing, and keep pushing into the future always.

I believe the future will be very bright. I hope you choose to have that belief also - faith centered and family centered.

I had an English teacher once say to the class on the first day, "Some of you have heard I am a very hard teacher – the hardest teacher they will ever have. They were right! Some of you have heard I am a very easy teacher. They were right, as well. What is it that you will choose to believe?"

… So what is it that you will choose to believe – and do?

Charles Farrior earned a bachelor's degree from Mississippi State University and an MBA from Mississippi College. He has provided solutions to customers in the defense industry for more than thirty years, has hired hundreds of employees, and has designed and/or improved business practices. He owns Charles Farrior Solutions, LLC, which is a management consulting firm; and Candy's Foods, which provides three BBQ "Q-Kick" sauces. Visit charlesfarriorsolutions.com and candysfoods.biz to learn more.

www.ingramcontent.com/pod-product-compliance
Lightning Source LLC
Chambersburg PA
CBHW030754180526
45163CB00003B/1022